# COLOR SHUFFLE
## new quilts from karla alexander

*Martingale*®
& COMPANY

# acknowledgments

I would like to acknowledge the following people and extend my sincere thanks to each one of them:

My wholehearted appreciation to my husband, friend, and soul mate, Don, who supports, encourages, feeds, and puts up with me. He definitely deserves the "Crazy Quilter's Husband Extraordinaire Lifetime Award" for always being there for me!

Sally Blankenship, who is an amazing quilt artist and who was always available to lend a hand with binding, offer ideas, and assist me as my deadline approached. I have a tremendous amount of appreciation for her and treasure our friendship.

Sylvia Dorney, owner of Greenbaum's Quilted Forest, for her continued support and willingness to work with me regardless of my hectic schedule. I enjoy and value our friendship.

A special thanks to my editors—Mary V. Green, Tina Cook, Robin Strobel, Melissa Bryan, as well as Stan Green, Shelly Garrison, Adrienne Smitke, and the entire Martingale staff.

Color Shuffle: New Quilts from Karla Alexander
© 2009 by Karla Alexander

That Patchwork Place® is an imprint of
Martingale & Company®.

Martingale & Company
20205 144th Avenue NE
Woodinville, WA 98072-8478
www.martingale-pub.com

Printed in China
14 13 12 11 10 09          8 7 6 5 4 3 2 1

**Library of Congress Cataloging-in-Publication Data
is available upon request.**

ISBN: 978-1-56477-927-4

## credits

President & CEO: Tom Wierzbicki
Editor in Chief: Mary V. Green
Managing Editor: Tina Cook
Developmental Editor: Karen Costello Soltys
Technical Editor: Robin Strobel
Copy Editor: Melissa Bryan
Design Director: Stan Green
Production Manager: Regina Girard
Illustrator: Adrienne Smitke
Cover & Text Designer: Shelly Garrison
Photographer: Brent Kane

## mission statement

Dedicated to providing quality products and service to inspire creativity

# CONTENTS

# INTRODUCTION

Quilts have been made for many generations and have become a major passion of mine. In designing the quilts for this book, it has been my goal to encourage quilters of all ages and abilities to quilt and create memories for generations to come.

What often lingers in my mind are the fond memories I have as a young girl helping my mom with her hand quilting. First I retrieved the boards and quilting basket filled with clamps; a mason jar full of tacks, pins, and needles; snipped-off rubber-glove fingers for grabbing needles; and slivers of soap for marking quilt lines. Mom joined two-by-four boards with simple C-clamps to form a frame. Next she carefully tacked the quilt to the frame. Days would pass with the noise of the TV muffled, hidden behind the quilt contraption.

My mom always encouraged me to help and, surprisingly, never removed any of my rogue stitches (as far as I'm aware). What I enjoyed most was hiding underneath the tightly stretched quilt. I loved to watch the stitches magically appear, eventually forming long lines. As the days wore on, the quilt was rolled smaller and smaller as it neared completion. Soon I would be back in demand when it came time to remove the tacks with a butter knife.

Fast-forward and here I am working on my fifth quilt book, thanks in part to my days spent underneath the frame of a quilt top. I am so grateful to my mom and the memories she had no idea she was creating. Although the back of the quilt was often my favorite, I still recall the multitude of gingham, polka-dot, and plaid fabrics she used in her quilts. I suppose it's no surprise that I have a difficult time using only three or four fabrics for one quilt! In my opinion the more fabrics the merrier, but now it's by choice and not necessity. So explore the projects in this book, grab your fabrics, and enjoy the journey while creating your own memories.

# QUILTMAKING BASICS

To make good-quality quilts, you need to use good-quality equipment. A sewing machine in proper working order, high-quality supplies and tools, and accuracy in stitching are all crucial. The better your equipment, the less distracted and more productive you will be.

## TOOLS AND SUPPLIES

The following basic tools and techniques are necessary to make the quilts in this book.

**Acrylic rulers.** You can never have too many rulers. For the projects in this book, however, I suggest a few basic sizes. A 6" x 24" ruler is great for cutting long strips, and square rulers are essential for cutting squares and trimming up pieced blocks. A 12½" x 12½" ruler works for projects with blocks 12½" and smaller, but I also love the smaller sizes, such as 9½" x 9½".

**Cutting mat.** My favorite size is 24" x 35", but a 17" x 23" mat works well if space is an issue.

**Mounting tape.** I tape this on my sewing machine to use as a guide when sewing curves. This is a double-sided tape with foam backing that comes on a roll. If you're concerned about any residue the tape might leave on the bed of your sewing machine, place a piece of blue painter's tape down first.

**Quilting thread.** Choosing your quilting thread is one of the last decisions to be made. I use a variety of threads, from cotton to silky rayon and metallic. I always use the best-quality thread available.

**Rotary cutter.** Start each new project with a sharp new blade that will allow you to cut through several layers of fabric at a time.

**Sewing machine.** Always be kind to your sewing machine—keep it in good working order, change needles as necessary, and keep it free of lint.

**Sewing thread.** Use good-quality, 100%-cotton thread. I tend to use neutral colors for piecing my blocks.

**Spray sizing.** I have become a huge fan of spray sizing. I find it helps fight distortion and keeps the edges of my pieces nice and crisp.

## the 10-foot rule

If you're purchasing new fabric, stack the bolts of fabric, one on top of another, on the counter or stand them side by side. If you're working from your stash, fold and stack the fabrics on your worktable and fan them out. Then back up approximately 10 feet and take a look. Do the fabrics contrast well with one another? Does one fabric jump out from the rest? If so, it may need a "companion." For example, if you have just one red fabric in the mix and your eye goes right to it every time you look at the stack, try adding another red (or two) to the mix for a better balance.

On the other hand, if you have three fabrics from the same color group, use the 10-foot rule to determine if they appear to blend together too much, resembling a single piece of fabric. Instead of having three medium blues that all muddle together, swap one out for a brighter blue, a blue that has another color in the print, or something else to liven up the group.

One of my favorite tools for evaluating fabric is a simple door peephole, available at any home-improvement center. Looking through a peephole distances you from your fabric choices and helps you determine if you have a "jumper" (a fabric that jumps out at you) or too many fabrics that blend together. Also now available at most quilt stores is a fabric-reducing tool, which looks a lot like a magnifying glass. It is much larger than the door peephole, making the viewing process even easier.

# FABRIC CHOICES

Often one of the most challenging parts of making a quilt can be choosing the fabric. I usually go about this by deciding on a fabric theme, or how I envision the quilt to look once it's complete. I usually choose between batiks, soft or bold colors, bright prints with funky designs or traditional polka dots, plaids, and so on. I always apply my "10-foot rule" (explained on page 5) before making my final choice.

Before beginning a quilt, I always check my stash to see if there is something I already own and can use. If you look closely at the photographs, you will probably detect that some of the quilts contain more fabrics than the instructions call for. With many of the projects in this book, it's easy to throw a few extra fabrics into the mix just to spice things up. Challenge yourself to go through your stash and use some of your leftovers—I did!

# STACK THE DECK BLOCKS

Some of the quilts in this book use my "stack the deck" technique. With this method you stack fabric squares or rectangles into a "deck" and then slice the deck into various shapes, either curved or straight. The order of the fabrics is shuffled and the pieces sewn together. I like to use this method because it gives me the advantage of using many different fabrics without having to mess around with a lot of math. If you want more blocks than the pattern calls for, you can usually start with as many squares or rectangles as you would like completed blocks. This makes it easy to go to your stash and find a few pieces of a favorite fabric that is nearly gone. As long as you can cut it into a square or rectangle as required in the quilt pattern, you can usually use it. I like that option!

## stacking the fabric decks

Once you cut the initial number of squares or rectangles required, stack the number of pieces indicated in the pattern right side up for rotary cutting. Alternate colors as directed for each individual quilt. Stack the squares or rectangles as perfectly as you can with the edges even. Make sure you haven't duplicated the same fabric in any one deck unless directed to do so. Keep in mind that in most decks, the top fabric will

eventually be moved to the bottom of the deck, so it's also a good idea to make sure that sufficient contrast exists between the top and bottom fabrics.

## slicing the decks

Once your decks are neatly stacked and ready to go, use your rotary cutter and ruler to cut the deck in pieces as directed.

Refer to the illustration for each project and use a chalk marker to draw the cutting lines directly onto the fabric deck. This is easy to do, and you can brush the lines away if you don't like the outcome and redraw until you do. Unless otherwise noted, you can vary the lines from one deck to the next. This gives each deck its own individual style.

## shuffling the decks

Shuffling simply means rearranging the fabric segments once they have been cut. By shuffling each stack of fabric in a specific number and order, you will create the correct arrangement of fabrics in each block. Each project will give instructions on which stacks and how many pieces to shuffle.

Top fabric shuffled to bottom of stack

Top two fabrics shuffled to bottom of stack

One stack unshuffled

Top three fabrics shuffled to bottom of stack

## preparing a paper layout

Once you have completed the shuffling process, reassemble the block and pin each stack of segments to a piece of paper through all layers. Be sure to keep the segments in the exact order and position in which you shuffled them. Once the segments are secure, use a pencil and trace along the cutting lines onto the paper. The pins will help keep the segments in order and the lines will create a template reference.

## chain piecing

Use chain piecing as directed in the project. Chain piece by flipping piece 2 onto piece 1 with right sides together and then sewing along the edge. Without breaking the thread, sew pieces 1 and 2 from the next layer together. Continue with each layer, sewing piece 1 to piece 2 without breaking the thread in between.

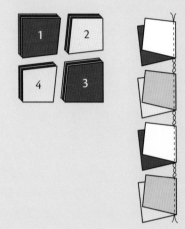

In some of the projects you can continue to sew segments to the chain-pieced units without cutting the threads between them. The instructions will let you know if this is an option. After the segments are sewn together, press the seams as indicated, cut the units apart, and restack them in the exact order they were before sewing. Press the seams as necessary. Continue adding segments together in numerical order; then sew together combined units as directed.

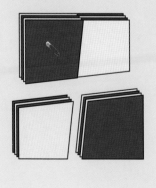

## sewing the blocks

Sew the blocks as directed with each project. Usually the sewing order is the exact opposite order of how the segments were cut. It's important to keep the segment stacks in their shuffled order while sewing; otherwise you'll end up unintentionally duplicating a fabric within a block. I strongly recommend that you place a safety pin in the top layer of the first segment to be sewed. This way, if you're chain piecing you will always know which pieces belong to the top layer and that the combined sewed segments are in the correct sequence.

## trimming

In some of the projects, segments will need to be trimmed before they are sewn. This is due to seam allowances; the pieced segments shrink up and are smaller than the unpieced segment they will be added to. Trim the excess fabric as directed to even the edges for the next piece.

Blocks with a lot of seams or that have curves may end up different sizes or become distorted and "out of square." If this happens, you can often trim the blocks, making the quilt assembly much easier. If size is not critical, trim to the size of your smallest block. Place a square ruler on top of the block and trim two sides. Align the trimmed edges with the correct measurement line on the ruler and trim the remaining two sides.

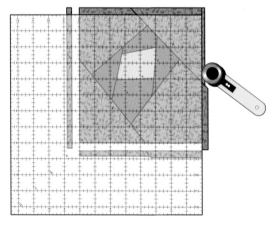

### curves

First, I always treat fabric with spray sizing when sewing curves. Choose your favorite brand of sizing to stabilize your fabric pieces and to help increase your accuracy. When cutting curves, always use your ruler by gently releasing the pressure and letting it gently slide into a curve. Let the ruler travel with your rotary cutter, sliding it across the surface of the fabric.

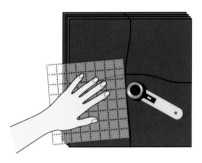

I also mark the center of the curve on both pieces and pin to keep them aligned for sewing. I find it much easier to sew curves by creating a seam guide with mounting tape on the bed of my sewing machine (see "Tools and Supplies" on page 5). Press a 1" to 2" strip of tape with the side edge exactly ¼" from the needle, extending it in front of the presser foot as shown.

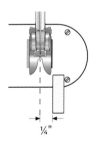

¼"

### variations

Many of the projects in this book allow for variations to the original design. I like to encourage you to create your own work and hopefully the designs in this book will help you on your way. Try to allow your quilt to evolve as you go. Change it up if you like by adding borders, different colors, or even more blocks. Take into account the size of your quilt and what you would like to use it for, make changes along the way, and enjoy.

I like to compare the quilts in this book to making soup. Keep adding to the mix until you're pleased. Whether you add borders, more colors, more blocks, or a screaming off-the-wall color for a binding—make it your own and work with it until you are happy!

## ASSEMBLING THE QUILT TOP

Once all your blocks are complete, it's time for the layout. Arrange your blocks in rows according to the project directions (or use your own arrangement). Play with the blocks—twisting, turning, and substituting them—until you're satisfied. I try to separate identical prints so that they don't end up next to each other in the finished quilt. View your arrangement from a distance using my "10-foot rule" (page 5) to check the visual balance.

Join your blocks into rows, matching the seams between the blocks. I like to pin each row to prevent any surprises once I'm done. Press seam allowances in the opposite direction from row to row so that opposing seams butt against each other. Join the rows of blocks into sets of two rows, and then sew the sets together.

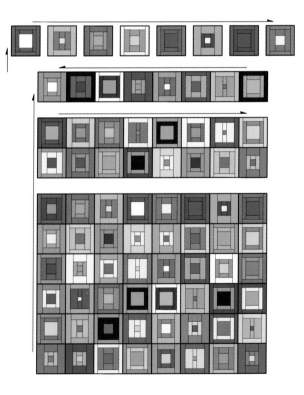

## BORDERS

Many of the quilts in this book are borderless. I chose this option because I truly believe a border or borders should make a quilt better and more beautiful, not just bigger! So if you find an awesome print that will make your quilt look that much more fabulous, go for it and add a border.

1. For each quilt that has a border, refer to the project's cutting directions and cut the required number of border strips.

2. Remove the selvages and sew the border strips together end to end to make one long strip. Press the seam allowances to one side.

3. Fold the long border strip in half lengthwise, matching short ends. Vertically center the folded border directly under the quilt top. Make sure the border and the quilt top are smooth without any wrinkles or pleats. Trim the doubled border strip even with the edges of the quilt top.

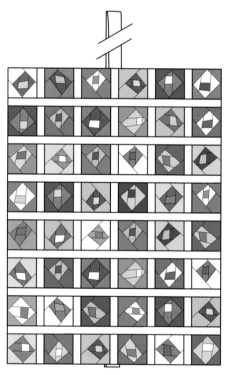

Trim border strip even with
quilt top and bottom.

4. Mark the halfway point of the border length and quilt top with a pin. Pin the borders to opposite sides of the quilt, matching center marks and ends. Sew the borders in place, easing in any fullness. Press seam allowances toward the borders.

5. Repeat steps 3 and 4, centering the border strip horizontally under the quilt top, to cut and add the top and bottom borders.

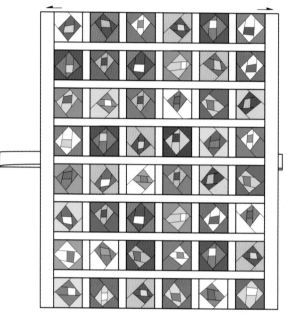

Trim border strip even with quilt sides.

## FINISHING THE QUILT

Once your quilt is completed, you will need to assemble it into a "quilt sandwich," which consists of the backing, batting, and quilt top. The quilt batting and backing should always be at least 4" to 6" larger than the quilt top.

1. Spread the backing wrong side up on a flat surface. Anchor it with pins or masking tape.

2. Spread the batting over the backing, smoothing out any wrinkles.

3. Center the quilt top on the batting.

## basting

For hand quilting, baste with a needle and thread. Start in the center and work diagonally, corner to corner, with large stitches. Next, baste in a grid, stitching horizontal and vertical rows across the quilt top. Space the rows approximately 6" apart. Finish by stitching all around the quilt perimeter.

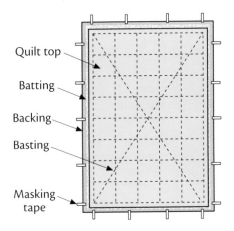

Quilt top
Batting
Backing
Basting
Masking tape

Pin baste if you plan to machine quilt. Pin basting is done most easily if you have a large table for laying out the quilt. Place 1" rustproof safety pins every 5" to 6" across the quilt top, beginning in the center and working your way to the outer edges. Place the pins where they won't interfere with the stitches of your planned quilting design.

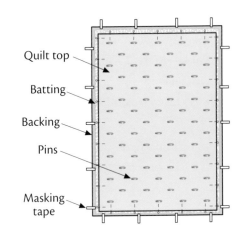

Quilt top
Batting
Backing
Pins
Masking tape

## quilting

Now is the time to give some attention to choosing a quilting design. I make the decision based on several factors. I consider the size of the quilt and whether it is something I can handle, and I also think about the design itself—whether the quilt is intense, simply need-ing a quilt pattern that won't detract from the design, or whether it would benefit from a fancy quilt pattern. Study your quilt and imagine how you would like the finished product to look. I often quilt small quilts using the "stitch-in-the-ditch" method, in which the quilting lines are stitched into the patch seam lines so that the quilting stitches are practically invisible on the right side of the patchwork. Quilts that are larger and more difficult to manage I often send a professional long-arm quilter.

## binding

Binding finishes the edges of your quilt. I prefer a double-fold, straight-grain binding, often referred to as a French-fold binding. I preview my choices by placing a folded edge under the quilt top, peeking out just enough so that it shows me how the binding would look. If I don't want the binding to stand out too much, I choose a color similar to the border (or, in the event there is no border, similar to the blocks). See "Blue Moon" on page 12 for an example. Other times I like to use a totally new color to liven things up a bit, as in the quilt "Shaken Not Stirred" on page 46. I very rarely choose the binding ahead of time, preferring to wait until I see how the quilt looks and then preview my choices at that time. Don't forget to use the "10-foot rule" on page 5 to check out your binding options and see how they look to you.

To make double-fold binding:

1. Trim the batting and backing even with the quilt top.

2. Refer to the cutting list for each individual project and cut the required number of binding strips.

3. Remove the selvages and place the strips right sides together as shown. Sew the strips together with diagonal seams to make one long binding strip. Trim the excess fabric, leaving a ¼" seam allowance, and press the seam allowances open to reduce bulk.

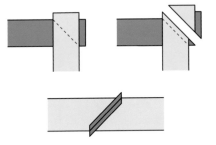

4. Fold the strip in half lengthwise, wrong sides together, and press.

5. I always use my walking foot when attaching binding. Beginning about 18" from a corner, place the binding right sides together with the quilt top. Align the raw edges. Leave a 10" tail and use a ¼" seam allowance to sew the binding to the front of your quilt. Stop sewing ¼" from the first corner and carefully backstitch two or three stitches. Clip the thread and remove the quilt from the machine.

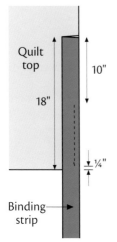

6. Rotate the quilt 90° so that you can work on the next side. Fold the binding up, creating a 45° angle, and then back down, even with the second side of the quilt. A little pleat will form at the corner.

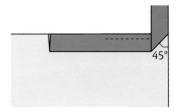

7. Resume stitching at the folded edge of the binding as shown. Continue stitching the binding to the quilt, turning the corners as described, until you are approximately 10" from the point at which you started sewing the binding. Remove the quilt from the sewing machine.

Fold

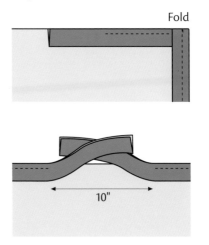

8. Fold back the beginning and ending tails of the binding strips so that they meet in the center of the unsewn portion of the quilt edge. Finger-press the folded edges.

9. Unfold both ends of the binding and match the center points of the two finger-pressed folds, forming an X as shown. Pin and sew the two ends together on the diagonal of the fold lines. Trim the excess binding ¼" from the seam. Finger-press the new seam allowances open and refold the binding. Finish sewing the binding to the quilt.

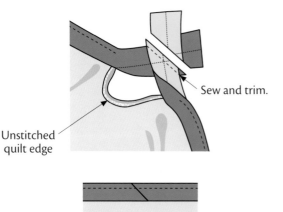

Sew and trim.

Unstitched quilt edge

10. Fold the binding over the edge of the quilt top to the back of the quilt, making sure to cover the machine stitching. Hand sew the binding in place, mitering the corners as you go.

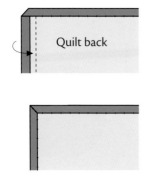

Quilt back

# BLUE MOON

This design-as-you-go quilt is so much fun to make. You can audition moon colors and sizes along the way, providing the opportunity to make changes well into the project. If you happen to have small pieces of one or two awesome prints that you would like to use—you can! I'd like to encourage you to take some liberty with my design and add more fabrics than the minimum listed in the instructions.

## MATERIALS

*All yardages are based on 42"-wide fabric.*

3/8 yard *each* of 8 different medium blue batiks for blocks

3/8 yard *each* of 8 different dark blue batiks for pieced border

1/3 yard *each* of 7 different light to medium lime green batiks for moons

2/3 yard of binding fabric

5 1/8 yards of backing fabric

70" x 90" piece of batting

Freezer paper

### fabric tips

I chose batik fabrics from a dreamy blue palette with a touch of turquoise for the background blocks. For the border I used darker blue batiks pieced into Four Patch blocks as a frame. For the moons, I used a variety of bright green prints as well as the medium and dark blue batiks.

Finished Quilt: 60" x 80"  •  Finished Block: 48 blocks, 10" x 10"
Machine quilted by SueAnn Suderman

# CUTTING

*All measurements include ¼" seam allowances.*

**From *each* of the medium blue batiks, cut:**
1 strip, 10⅞" x 42"; cut each strip into 3 squares, 10⅞" x 10⅞" (24 total)

**From *each* of the dark blue batiks, cut:**
1 strip, 11" x 42"; cut each strip into 3 squares, 11" x 11" (24 total)

**From the binding fabric, cut:**
8 strips, 2½" x 42"

# MAKING THE BACKGROUND BLOCKS

Refer to "Stack the Deck Blocks" on page 6 as needed.

1. Arrange the medium blue squares right side up in six decks of four squares each. Each deck should contain a different mix of fabrics. Secure each deck with a pin through all the layers until ready to work.

2. Work with one deck at a time and make sure the edges are all perfectly aligned. Cut through all four layers, corner to corner as shown, creating half-square triangles.

3. Shuffle the order of the triangles by moving the top triangle of one stack to the bottom of that stack.

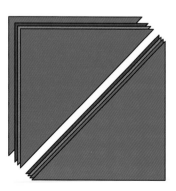

4. Sew the half-square triangles together. Press the seam allowances in one direction.

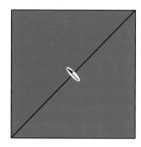

5. Repeat steps 2–4 until all 24 medium blue blocks are sewn.

# MAKING THE BORDER BLOCKS

1 Arrange the dark blue squares right side up into four decks of six layers each. Each deck should contain a different mix of fabrics. Secure each deck with a pin through all the layers until ready to work.

2. Work with one deck at a time and make sure the edges are all perfectly aligned. Cut through all six layers 5½" from each side vertically and horizontally to create 5½" squares. Separate the squares into four small stacks as shown.

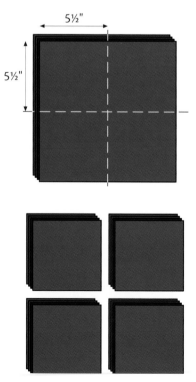

3. Shuffle the deck by taking the top square from the upper-left stack and placing it on the bottom of that stack. Take the top two squares from the upper-right stack and place them on the bottom of that stack. Take the top three squares from the lower-right stack and place them on the bottom of that stack. Leave the lower-left stack of squares unshuffled.

4. Working with the upper two stacks, chain sew the top left and right squares together. (See "Chain Piecing" on page 7.) Without cutting the thread, continue sewing the remaining five layers until all the upper squares are sewn. Press seam allowances to one side. Cut threads, stack the units in the exact order in which they were sewn, and set aside.

5. Repeat step 4 and chain sew the bottom left and right squares together. Press seam allowances in the opposite direction of the top unit. Cut threads and stack the units in the exact order in which they were sewn.

6. Chain sew the top and bottom units together to make six Four Patch blocks. Press the seam allowances in one direction.

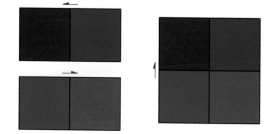

7. Repeat steps 2–6 for the remaining decks to make 24 Four Patch blocks.

## MAKING THE MOONS

1. Measure the medium blue half-square-triangle blocks as well as the dark blue Four Patch blocks. It's imperative that the blocks are exactly the same size. If they are not, use a square acrylic ruler to trim to the same size. It's OK if they don't measure the same as mine (10½"), as long as they are all the same size.

2. Arrange the medium blue blocks into four vertical rows of six blocks each. Place the dark blue Four Patch blocks around the outside edges in the border position. Rotate the blocks until you're happy with the design, making sure that identical prints aren't side by side. Do not sew the blocks together at this time.

## karla's tip

I like to use spray sizing when I cut and sew curves. Also, take an extra step to find the exact ¼" seam allowance for your sewing machine.

3. To make templates, trace each pattern on pages 18–21 onto the paper side of freezer paper, marking the center point of the curve. Cut out the templates on the tracing lines. The moons are three different sizes. Each size moon has a quarter-circle template for cutting the moon and a different quarter-circle background template for cutting the pieced block background. Make six or seven templates for each of the moons and backgrounds. Templates can be reused a couple of times. Just peel off the last piece of fabric and re-press the template to the next fabric.

4. Using a hot, dry iron, press a moon quarter-circle template shiny side down on the right side of a lime green batik. Use scissors or your rotary cutter to cut the quarter circle flush with the template, snipping a tiny ¹⁄₁₆" nick to mark the center point of the curve. From the variety of lime green batiks, cut 24 quarter circles for the A moons, 16 quarter circles for the B moons, and 10 quarter circles for the C moons.

5. Arrange the lime green quarter circles on top of the half-square-triangle blocks to create the circle "moons," making certain identical prints are not side by side and using the same size quarter circles in each moon. For the blue moons, cut additional quarter circles from the leftover medium and dark blue batiks, or work as you go and use the medium and dark blue quarter circles cut from the half-square-triangle and Four Patch blocks from step 9 on page 17. Cut 10 medium blue and 8 dark blue moon B quarter circles, and 4 medium blue and

4 dark blue moon C quarter circles. Swap colors around and switch in different fabrics from your stash until you're happy with the placement. I had fun placing a few half circles on the edges and swapping a couple of the dark and medium blue fabrics. You may end up with an entirely different arrangement!

6. Work on one block at a time and mark the upper-left corner of each block with a safety pin to prevent incorrect rotation.

7. Begin with moon A quarter circles. Arrange and pin in place on the blocks.

8. Remove one block at a time from the layout. Position a moon A background template in the corner of the block where you will sew the quarter circle, matching the corner and edges as shown. Press in place using a hot, dry iron.

9. Use scissors or a rotary cutter to carefully cut around the background template, flush with the edges. Snip a tiny ¹⁄₁₆" cut to mark the center of the curve. Peel off the paper template. You can save the cutout half circle to make some of the blue moons in step 5 on page 16.

10. Right sides together, pin the background on top of the quarter circle, matching edges and center marks as shown below. (Placing the quarter circle on the bottom and the background on top will make sewing the curve easier.) Pin, matching the curved edges and using as many pins as you like. Refer to "Curves" on page 8 as needed.

11. Using a scant ¼" seam allowance, sew carefully along the curve. If needed, make tiny pivots with the needle in the down position. Press the seam allowance toward the quarter circle. Place the block back in the layout.

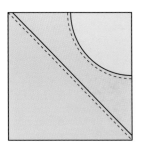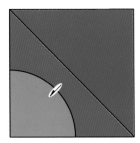

12. Repeat steps 6–11 until all the moon A quarter circles are sewn to the background blocks. Next, cut and sew the moon B and moon C quarter circles to their backgrounds. You may notice that my quilt has a blue half-moon at the lower-right corner. I opened one of the background block seams, sewed the quarter circles, and reassembled the Four Patch.

### karla's tip

If you want to make moons the same size as shown in the diagram, cut the quarter circles as directed. If you would like some of the moons in different sizes, cut the quarter circles for the moons with a radius ¼" larger than the desired finished size. Cut the quarter circle for the background with a radius ¼" smaller than the desired finished size (or ½" smaller than the cut size of the quarter-circle moon).

## ASSEMBLY

Refer to "Assembling the Quilt Top" on page 8 for guidance as needed. Pin and sew the blocks together into six vertical rows; press seam allowances in alternate directions from row to row. Make a ⅛" nick in a seam allowance if you need to release one of the allowances so they will alternate. Sew the rows together.

## FINISHING

Refer to "Finishing the Quilt" on page 9 as needed.

1. Cut the backing fabric crosswise into two panels, each approximately 90" long. Remove the selvages and sew the pieces together along a long edge to make a backing approximately 70" x 90". Press the seam allowance to one side.

2. Layer the quilt top with the batting and backing, with the backing seam parallel to the long edges of the quilt top. Baste the layers together using your favorite method.

3. Hand or machine quilt as desired.

4. Trim the backing and batting even with the edges of the quilt top and use the 2½"-wide strips to bind the quilt.

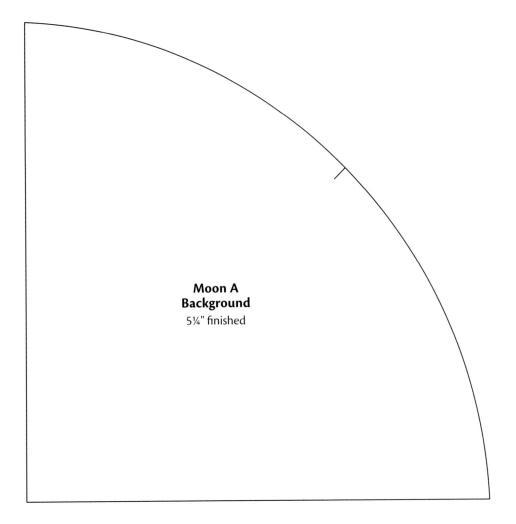

**Moon A**
**Background**
5¼" finished

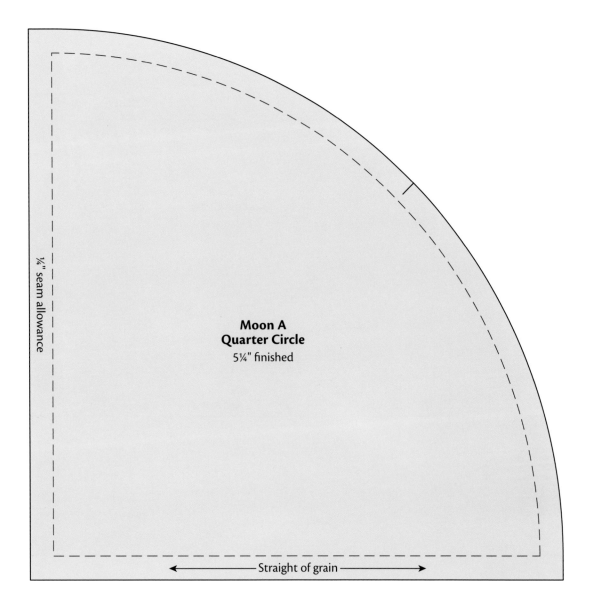

**Moon A
Quarter Circle**
5¼" finished

¼" seam allowance

Straight of grain

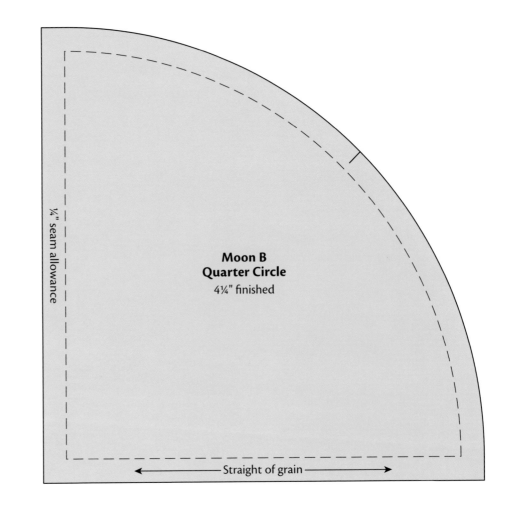

**Moon B
Quarter Circle**
4¼" finished

¼" seam allowance

←———— Straight of grain ————→

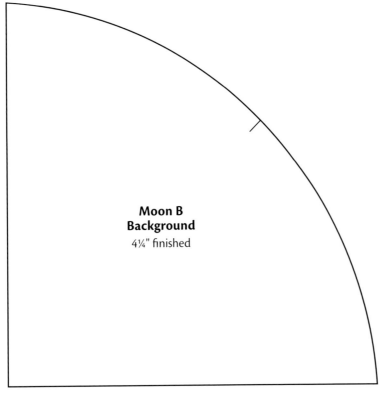

**Moon B
Background**
4¼" finished

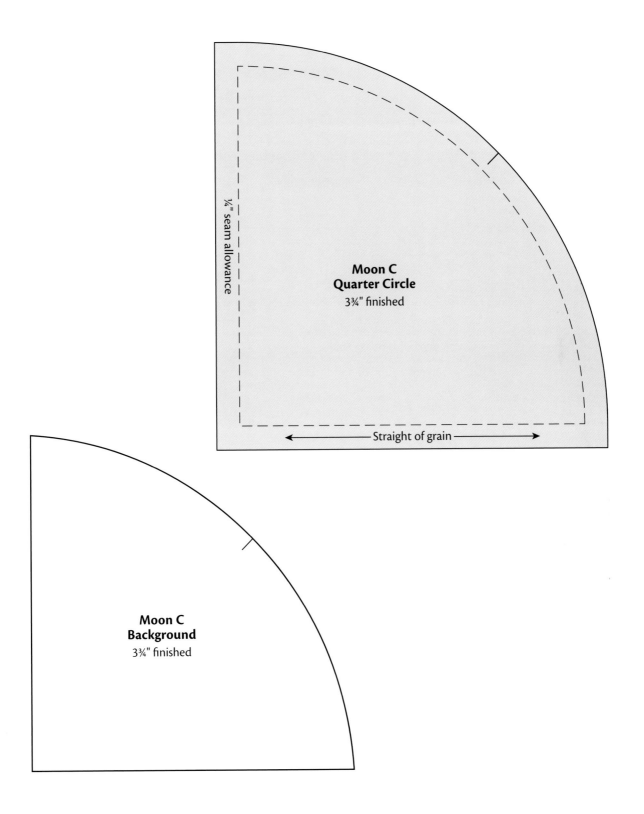

**Moon C
Quarter Circle**
3¾" finished

¼" seam allowance

← Straight of grain →

**Moon C
Background**
3¾" finished

# Window Box

Have you ever received a gift that you had to keep opening and opening and the boxes got ever smaller? This is the fabric version of that—but you get to be in charge of the boxes and decide how big each one is. My Stack the Deck technique makes it easy and fun and also gives you the surprise of what happens when the blocks are placed together.

Try making this quilt with a different-sized square (6" x 6" or bigger), enjoy a new palette of prints, or create your own stash challenge.

## MATERIALS

*All yardages are based on 42"-wide fabric.*

80 assorted 10" x 10" squares, or ⅜ yard each of 20 different contrasting prints

⅔ yard of binding fabric

4⅞ yards of backing fabric

70" x 85" piece of batting

## fabric tips

Have you noticed one of the great new marketing techniques the fabric companies are using, which allows you to purchase a piece of each fabric in an entire line without having to empty your entire savings account? The 10" x 10" square packets, sometimes called "layer cakes," are great for this project. I bought two layer cakes of the same fabric collection. Each set yielded 40 squares, so I ended up with 80 squares, which was perfect for this project.

Preview fabric for this quilt by standing bolts of fabric side by side, or arrange choices over the back of a couch or on your design wall if you have one. Move them around and use my "10-foot rule" (page 5) to make sure you have contrast with the light and dark values. Not every stack has to be a perfect balance of light and dark, though—that's what gives this little quilt its charm. The more contrast you have, the sharper the design. If your choices don't have a lot of contrast, your quilt will have a soft, blended look. It would also be striking made entirely out of solid fabrics.

Finished Quilt: 60" x 75" • Finished Block: 80 blocks, 7½" x 7½"
Pieced by Karla Alexander, quilted by Dave Suderman

## CUTTING

*All measurements include ¼" seam allowances.*

From *each* of the 20 different contrasting prints, cut:
1 strip, 10" x 42"; cut each strip into 4 squares,
   10" x 10" (80 total)

From the binding fabric, cut:
7 strips, 2½" x 42"

## ABOUT THE BLOCKS

Refer to "Stack the Deck Blocks" on page 6 as needed.

Each block in this quilt is essentially a square in a square in a square, or three concentric squares. The width of fabric strips varies from one block to another—some have a chunky square in the middle surrounded by skinnier strips, while others have itty-bitty center squares surrounded by wider strips. I've provided a list of cut sizes I used, but you can use any combination you like. Below are a few pointers:

- Pretreat squares with your favorite spray sizing to help prevent distortion while sewing.

- To balance the blocks, alternate contrasting prints when you layer each deck.

- Work with just one deck at a time. This way, you can examine your cuts and determine how you want to cut the next deck.

- The decks are cut in two "rounds," which will be labeled from the center outward in the sewing order. This is the opposite of the cutting order. In the diagram below, the round numbers are blue and the piece letters are black.

| | R2 A | |
|---|---|---|
| | R1 A | |
| R2 B  R1 B | Center | R1 B  R2 B |
| | R1 A | |
| | R2 A | |

- Cut each deck differently, but at first, make the cuts in each round the same width. Once you're comfortable with the method, try cutting your decks with the middle square off-center and with different-sized cuts in each round.

- Here are some measurements to get you started cutting your decks. You can also use the second measurement for the first cut, and the first measurement for the second cut.

  - First cut: 1½"; second cut: 1½"
  - First cut: 2½"; second cut: 2"
  - First cut: 1½"; second cut: 2"
  - First cut: 1½"; second cut: 3½"

- One of the steps in constructing a block is to trim some of the strips. To begin, I suggest that you measure, trim, and sew each round separately. Once you're comfortable with the method, and if you have an exact ¼" seam allowance, you can trim all your rectangles to size before you sew. If you don't have an exact ¼" seam allowance, you will need to measure and trim each rectangle just before you sew it rather than ahead of time.

## MAKING THE BLOCKS

1. Arrange the 10" x 10" squares, right sides up, into 20 decks of four squares each, alternating contrasting prints. Each deck should have a different mix of fabric. Secure each deck with a pin through all the layers.

2. Work with one deck at a time, making sure the edges are all perfectly aligned before cutting. Make the first round of cuts, slicing 2" from both the right and left sides of the deck. Label the two stacks of rectangles "round 2B." Move the rectangles away from the deck and cut 2" from both the top and the bottom edges of the deck. Label the two stacks of rectangles "round 2A."

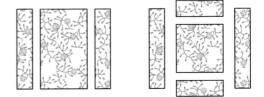

3. Cut the second round, slicing 2" from both the right and left sides of the stack of squares, and label the two stacks of rectangles "round 1B." Move them away from the stack and cut 2" from both the top and bottom edges of the deck. Label the two stacks of rectangles "round 1A."

4. Shuffle round 1A and round 1B stacks by peeling off the top fabric in each stack and placing it on the bottom of that stack. Take two layers from the top of the center stack and shuffle them to the bottom of that stack. Do not shuffle the round 2 stacks.

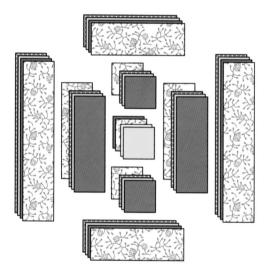

5. Chain piece round 1A rectangles to the top and then the bottom of the center squares. (See "Chain Piecing" on page 7.) Press seam allowances toward the rectangles and keep the units in the exact order in which they were shuffled.

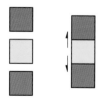

6. Measure the length of the units. Trim the round 1B rectangles to this exact length. If your seam allowance is a precise ¼", you will always trim 1" from the length of the round 1B rectangles regardless of how wide the rectangles were cut.

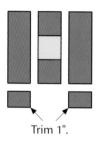

Trim 1".

7. Chain piece a trimmed round 1B rectangle to each long side of the four units from step 5. Press the seam allowances toward the rectangles and restack, keeping the units in the exact order in which they were shuffled.

8. Measure the width of the units; this will be the exact length to trim the round 2A rectangles. If your seam allowance is a precise ¼", you will always trim 1" from the length of the round 2A rectangles.

9. Chain piece trimmed round 2A rectangles to the top and bottom of the four units. Press the seams toward the rectangles and keep the units in the exact order in which they were shuffled.

10. Measure the width of the units; this will be the exact length to trim the round 2B rectangles. If your seam allowance is a precise ¼", you will always trim 2" from the length of the round 2B rectangles.

11. Chain piece trimmed round 2B rectangles to the sides of each of the four units. Press the seam allowances toward the rectangles.

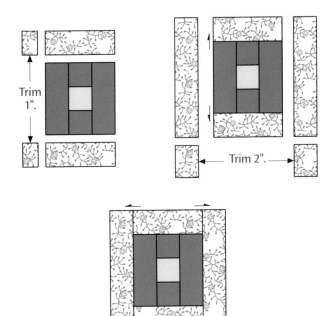

Make 80.

12. Repeat steps 2–11 for the remaining decks. Vary the width of the cuts for each deck. Make 80 blocks.

## ASSEMBLY

1. Arrange the blocks into eight vertical rows of 10 blocks each, making sure that identical prints are not side by side. View your arrangement from a distance using my "10-foot rule" (page 5) to check the visual balance.

2. Sew the blocks into rows. Press the seam allowances in alternating directions from row to row.

3. Sew the rows together into five segments of two each. Sew the segments together into one set of four rows and one set of six rows. Combine the sets. Press the seam allowances in one direction.

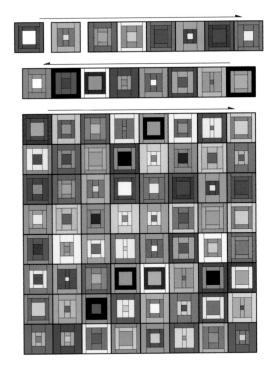

## FINISHING

Refer to "Finishing the Quilt" on page 9 as needed.

1. Divide the backing fabric crosswise into two equal panels, each approximately 85" long. Remove the selvages and sew the pieces together along a long edge to make a backing piece approximately 70" x 85"; press the seam allowances to one side.

2. Layer the quilt top with the batting and backing, keeping the backing seam parallel to the long edges of the quilt top. Baste the layers together using your favorite method.

3. Hand or machine quilt as desired. My quilt was long-arm quilted with a medium-sized stipple pattern.

4. Trim the backing and batting even with the edges of the quilt top and use the 2½"-wide strips to bind the quilt.

# HULLABALOO

This tricked-out quilt is a fast blast to make, and the pattern is great for working with anything from large-scale prints to photo transfers to T-shirt logos. You'll "stack the deck" with rectangles, and then balance them against a big block and sashing, arranging, blending, and balancing your colors as you go.

## MATERIALS

*All yardages are based on 42"-wide fabric.*

1⅔ yards of turquoise floral for blocks and border

½ yard *each* of 5 different blue and turquoise prints in a variety of small, medium, and large scales for blocks

⅜ yard *each* of 4 different blue and turquoise prints for sashing (can be the same as block fabrics if desired)

⅝ yard of binding fabric

5¼ yards of backing fabric

69" x 92" piece of batting

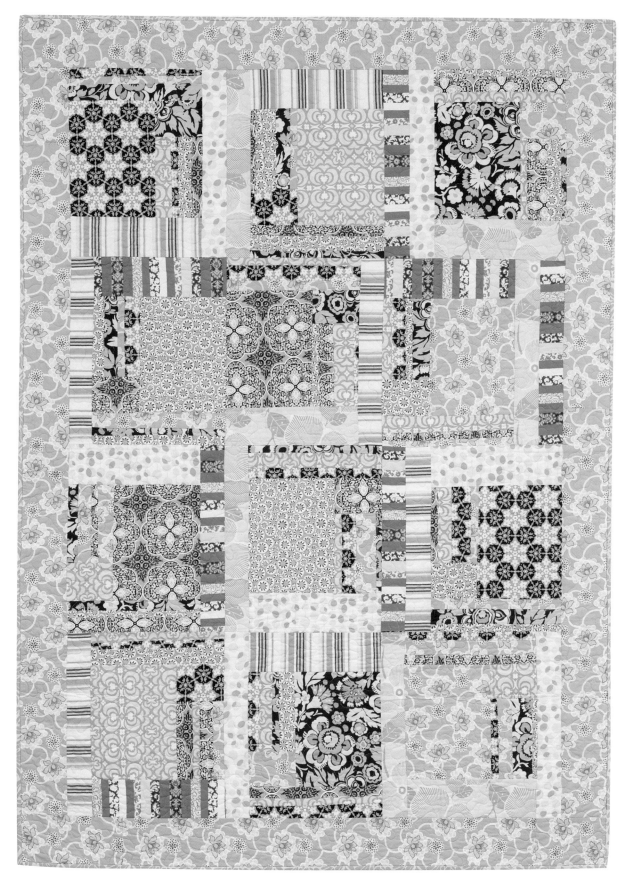

Finished Quilt: 61" x 82"   •   Finished Block: 12 blocks, 13" x 14"
Pieced by Karla Alexander, quilted by Dave Suderman

# CUTTING

*Refer to the illustration below for fabric placement.*
*All measurements include ¼" seam allowances.*

**From the turquoise floral, cut:**

2 A rectangles, 4½" x 13½"

2 B rectangles, 6½" x 8"

2 C rectangles, 4" x 5"

2 D rectangles, 9" x 11½"

7 strips, 5½" x 42"

**From *each* of the turquoise and blue prints for blocks, cut:**

2 A rectangles, 4½" x 13½" (10 total)

2 B rectangles, 6½" x 8" (10 total)

2 C rectangles, 4" x 5" (10 total)

2 D rectangles, 9" x 11½" (10 total)

**From *each* of the turquoise and blue prints for sashing, cut:**

1 strip, 4½" x 42"; cut each strip into 3 rectangles, 4½" x 13½" (12 total)

2 strips, 3 " x 42"; cut each strip into 2 rectangles, 3" x 18½" (16 total)

**From the binding fabric, cut:**

8 strips, 2½" x 42"

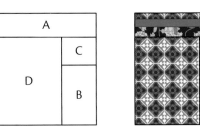

## MAKING THE BLOCKS

Refer to "Stack the Deck Blocks" on page 6 as needed.

1. Arrange and stack the A rectangles into three decks of four rectangles each. Each stack should have a different mix of fabrics. Secure each stack with a safety pin through all layers until ready to sew.

2. Work with one deck at a time. Use your ruler and rotary cutter to cut lengthwise through the deck twice to create three strips. Make each cut a different width from the next, no narrower than 1¼" and no wider than 2".

3. Shuffle the deck by peeling the top fabric off the top stack of strips and placing it on the bottom of that stack. Peel two layers from the top of the center stack and place them on the bottom of that stack.

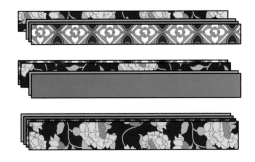

4. Starting with the top layer, chain piece the strips together by sewing all the top and center stacks together. (See "Chain Piecing" on page 7.) Open the units up and add the bottom strip to the first two. Press seam allowances to one side. Repeat with the other decks to make 12 strip units, each 13½" long.

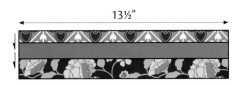

13½"

5. Repeat steps 1–4 with the B rectangles, cutting through each deck three times to make four strips. Make each cut a different width from the next, no narrower than 1½" and no wider than 2".

6. Shuffle the deck by peeling the top fabric off the first stack of strips and placing it on the bottom of that stack. Peel two layers from the top of the second stack of strips and move them to the bottom of that stack. Peel three layers from the top of the third stack and move them to the bottom of that stack. Do not shuffle the fourth stack.

7. Chain piece the strips together as in step 4. Press seam allowances to one side. Repeat with the other decks to make 12 strip units, each 8" long.

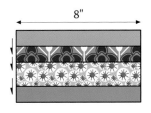

8"

8. Arrange an A unit, a B unit, a C rectangle, and a D rectangle as shown below. Repeat for the remaining blocks. Mix and match the pieces until you're happy with the arrangement for each block.

9. Pin and sew the C rectangles to the B strip units. Press the seam allowances toward the C rectangles.

10. Pin and sew the D rectangles to the combined B/C units. Press seam allowances toward the D rectangles.

11. Pin and sew the A units to the unit from step 10. Press seam allowances toward the A units.

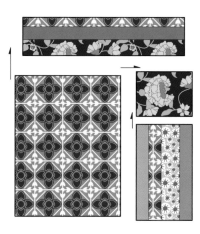

## ASSEMBLY

1. Arrange the blocks into four vertical rows of three blocks each. Leave room for the horizontal and vertical sashing. Switch and rotate the blocks around until you're satisfied with the layout. View your arrangement from a distance using the "10-foot rule" (page 5) to check the visual balance.

2. Arrange the 4½" x 13½" sashing strips horizontally on the top or bottom of each block. Arrange the 3" x 18½" sashing strips vertically between each of the blocks. I chose to arrange the vertical strips differently from row to row. Use the "10-foot rule" again to check the visual balance. Once you're satisfied with the layout, remove one block at a time and sew the horizontal sashing strip to each block. Press the seam allowances toward the sashing and replace the block back in the layout.

3. Sew the blocks and vertical sashing strips together in rows. Press seam allowances in opposite directions from row to row. Sew the rows together in pairs, and then sew the pairs together. Press seam allowances in one direction.

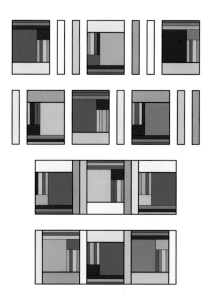

## ADDING BORDERS

Refer to "Borders" on page 9 as needed.

1. Sew the 5½" x 42" border strips together end to end to make one long strip.

2. Measure the length of the quilt top through the center and cut two border strips to this measurement.

3. Pin and sew the borders to the sides of the quilt. Press the seams toward the border strips.

4. Measure the width of the quilt top through the center, including the borders just added, and cut two border strips to this measurement.

5. Pin and sew the borders to the top and bottom of the quilt; press.

## FINISHING

Refer to "Finishing the Quilt" on page 9 as needed.

1. Divide the backing fabric crosswise into two equal panels, each approximately 94" long. Remove the selvages and sew the pieces together along the long edges to make a backing piece approximately 69" x 92"; press the seam allowances to one side.

2. Layer the quilt top with the batting and backing, keeping the backing seam parallel to the long edges of the quilt top. Baste the layers together using your favorite method.

3. Hand or machine quilt as desired. My quilt was long-arm quilted with a medium-sized stipple pattern.

4. Trim the backing and batting even with the edges of the quilt top and use the 2½"-wide strips to bind the quilt.

# THE SQUARE WITHIN

Bright colors make this cheerful quilt sparkle. I've always been somewhat square on the inside, and this quilt shows just how much fun that can be. And with such easy blocks, you'll be done piecing this quilt in no time at all.

## MATERIALS

*All yardages are based on 42"-wide fabric.*

⅔ yard *each* of 6 different dark red and purple prints for blocks

⅔ yard *each* of 6 different light green, pink, and yellow prints for blocks

⅝ yard of binding fabric

4¾ yards of backing fabric

63" x 84" piece of batting

### fabric tips

I chose medium- to large-scale, intensely colored prints for this quilt. I used my "10-foot rule" (page 5) to help determine which fabrics looked good together and had the strongest contrast. And, as with all my quilts, if I felt inspired to add another print into the mix—even midway through the quilt—I did it!

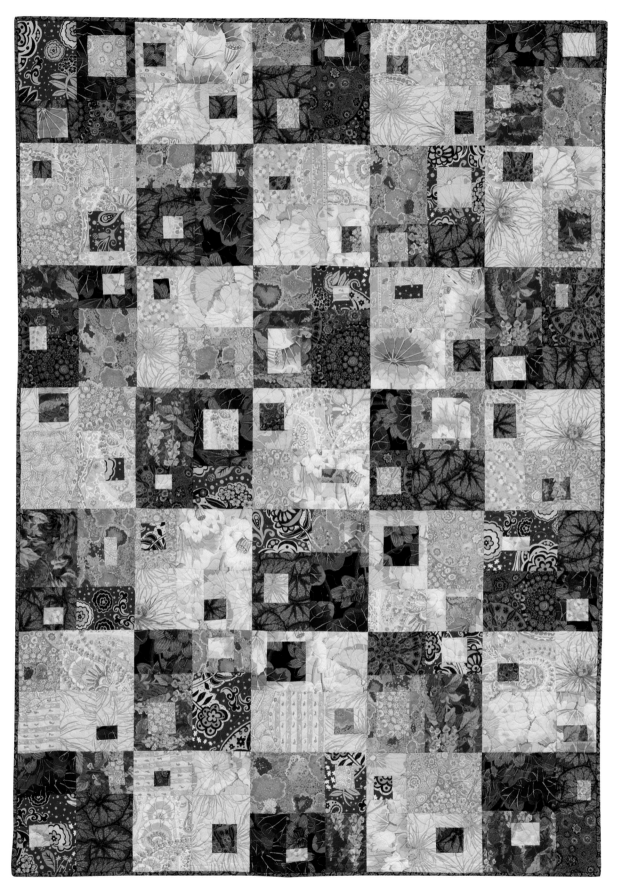

Finished Quilt: 52½" x 73½"  •  Finished Block: 35 blocks, 10½" x 10½"
Pieced by Karla Alexander, quilted by Dave Suderman

# CUTTING

*All measurements include ¼" seam allowances.*

**From *each* of the 6 dark red and purple prints, cut:**
1 strip, 6¾" x 42"; cut into:

    3 rectangles, 5½" x 6¾" (18 total)

    3 rectangles, 6¾" x 8" (18 total)

1 strip, 5¾" x 42"; cut into:

    3 rectangles, 5¾" x 7" (18 total)

    3 rectangles, 4½" x 5¾" (18 total)

**From *each* of the 6 light green, pink, and yellow prints, cut:**
1 strip, 6¾" x 42"; cut into:

    3 rectangles, 5½" x 6¾" (18 total)

    3 rectangles, 6¾" x 8" (18 total)

1 strip, 5¾" x 42"; cut into:

    3 rectangles, 5¾" x 7" (18 total)

    3 rectangles, 4½" x 5¾" (18 total)

**From the binding fabric, cut:**
7 strips, 2½" x 42"

# MAKING THE BLOCKS

Refer to "Stack the Deck Blocks" on page 6 as needed. You will find that the blocks assemble quickly, especially if you sew with an accurate ¼" seam allowance.

1. Randomly choose and neatly stack nine decks with four 5½" x 6¾" rectangles each, right side up, alternating the dark red and purple rectangles with the light green, yellow, and pink rectangles. Each deck should be different. Secure the decks with a pin through all layers until ready to cut.

2. Work with one deck at a time. Use a chalk pencil and draw two vertical and two horizontal lines on the top fabric. These will be the cutting lines separating the center square from the outer frame. The shortest distance a line should be from the edge of the fabric or between two cuts is 1½". Preview the drawn lines to see if you like how they look. Mainly you need to look at the square in the center and realize it will shrink by ½" after sewing. The pieces along the edges will shrink up as well, so make

sure they aren't too skinny. The chalk lines are easy to work with—if you don't like the position of your lines, simply erase and redraw them. Once you're comfortable with this method, you can cut the slices freestyle without premarking the lines.

3. Make first cuts parallel to the long sides of the deck and move the cut stacks out of the way. Make the second cuts perpendicular to the first and on the center stack only. Shuffle the center square by peeling the top fabric off the stack and placing it on the bottom of that stack.

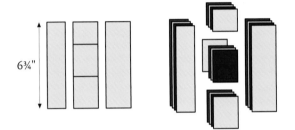

4. Starting with the top layer, chain stitch the small pieces to the center square as shown below. (See "Chain Piecing" on page 7.) Press seam allowances away from the center.

5. Measure the length of the unit from step 4. Trim the unsewn pieces to this exact length. If your seam allowance is an exact ¼", you will always trim 1". Chain stitch the last two pieces to opposite sides of the center unit. Press seam allowances toward the added pieces.

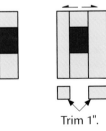

Trim 1".

6. Repeat steps 1–5 with all the decks to make 36 small blocks. Cut each deck different from the next, varying the size and shape of the center pieces.

7. Repeat steps 1–6 with the 6¾" x 8" rectangles to make 36 large blocks.

8. Separate the blocks with the light green, pink, or yellow outer edges from the blocks with the dark red and purple outer edges, keeping same sizes together.

9. Start with the blocks with dark edges. Randomly pair each small block with a dark 5¾" x 7" rectangle. (Choose a rectangle with a different fabric than is used in the block.) Sew the small blocks to the rectangles as shown below. Press seam allowances toward the rectangle. Repeat with the light-edge blocks and the light 5¾" x 7" rectangles to make 18 dark units and 18 light units.

Small block units.
Make 18 dark and 18 light.

10. Repeat step 9 with the large blocks and 4½" x 5¾" rectangles to make 18 dark units and 18 light units.

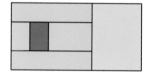

Large block units.
Make 18 dark and 18 light.

11. Randomly pair the dark units from step 9 with the dark units from step 10. Sew the pairs together into a jumbo block as shown. Repeat with the light units. Press seams to one side. You will have 18 dark jumbo blocks and 18 light jumbo blocks for a total of 36. If you arrange the blocks as in the quilt shown, you will have one block left over to use as a pillow or on the back of the quilt.

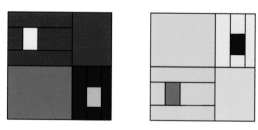

Jumbo block units.
Make 18 dark and 18 light.

## ASSEMBLY

1. Alternating light and dark, arrange the blocks into five horizontal rows of seven blocks each. Turn the blocks or move them around until you're satisfied with the arrangement. Use my "10-foot rule" to check for visual balance.

2. Sew the blocks together into rows. Press the seam allowances in opposite directions from row to row.

3. Sew the rows together and press the seam allowances in one direction.

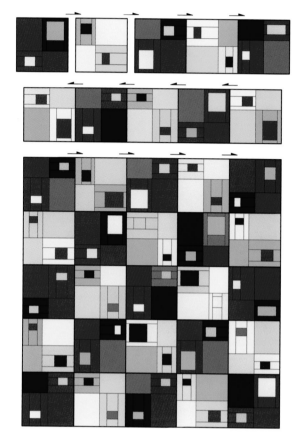

## FINISHING

Refer to "Finishing the Quilt" on page 9 as needed.

1. Divide the backing fabric crosswise into two equal panels, each approximately 85" long. Remove the selvages and sew the pieces together along a long edge to make a backing piece approximately 63" x 84". Press the seam allowances to one side.

2. Layer the quilt top with the batting and backing, keeping the backing seam perpendicular to the long edges of the quilt top. Baste the layers together using your favorite method.

3. Hand or machine quilt as desired. My quilt was long-arm quilted with a medium-sized stipple pattern.

4. Trim the backing and batting even with the edges of the quilt top and bind the quilt with the 2½"-wide strips.

# SOMERSAULT

Different-sized squares somersault down undulating paths created by wavy half-square triangles. You'll love the sneaky but simple technique used to create the corner squares. Experiment with changing the sizes and number of these squares—it's entirely up to you! With the alternating light and dark fabrics on the edges, I chose not to add a border, but that's another design option open to you.

## MATERIALS

*All yardages are based on 42"-wide fabric.*

⅜ yard *each* of 9 different light turquoise blue or purple prints for blocks

⅜ yard *each* of 9 different dark purplish blue prints for blocks

⅝ yard of binding fabric

3⅜ yards of backing fabric

59" x 80" piece of batting

### fabric tips

The colors I chose for this quilt were inspired by my love of the ocean. To get the flowing effect I was looking for, I chose fabrics that almost all have a subtle design. Using my "10-foot rule" (page 5), it's easy to choose fabric that appears as a solid from a distance but reveals its design when viewed up close. I chose an equal number of colors in light to medium and medium-dark values in a cool range of blues, turquoise, and purples. It's fun to pair the squares together to create a light and dark side. Sometimes a print that might be dark in one block will be light in another. It's your choice and makes your quilt unique. Then, when it's time to lay out your beautiful blocks, you can use the "10-foot rule" again to balance the entire quilt to your liking.

Finished Quilt: 49" x 70"  •  Finished Block: 70 blocks, 7" x 7"
Pieced by Karla Alexander, quilted by Dave Suderman

# CUTTING

*All measurements include ¼" seam allowances.*

**From *each* of the 9 different light turquoise blue or purple prints, cut:**

1 strip, 8" x 42"; cut into 4 squares, 8" x 8" (36 total; you will use only 35)

From the remaining yardage, cut:

11 total assorted squares, 3" x 3"

11 total assorted squares, 4" x 4"

**From *each* of the 9 different dark purplish blue prints, cut:**

1 strip, 8" x 42"; cut into 4 squares, 8" x 8" (36 total; you will use only 35)

From the remaining yardage, cut:

12 total assorted squares, 3" x 3"

13 total assorted squares, 4" x 4"

**From the binding fabric, cut:**

7 strips, 2½" x 42"

# MAKING THE BLOCKS

Refer to "Stack the Deck Blocks" on page 6 as needed.

1. Arrange the 35 light blue squares and 35 dark blue squares into 17 decks of 4 squares and 1 deck of 2 squares; each deck should contain different fabrics. Alternate dark squares with light squares, with the dark on top. Secure the decks with a pin through all layers until ready to sew.

2. Work with one deck at a time. Use a chalk marker to mark the top square diagonally, corner to corner in one direction. The chalk is easier to see if a dark square is on the top of the stack. Use your ruler to cut the first inch straight, exactly on the chalk line, and then release the pressure on your ruler and let it glide along with your rotary cutter to cut a gentle curve through the middle portion of the deck. (See "Curves" on page 8.) Straighten out the curve and cut exactly on the chalk line for the last inch.

3. Shuffle the upper-left fabric to the bottom of that stack. Starting with the top layer, sew the left and right triangles together. Press the seam allowances toward the dark triangles.

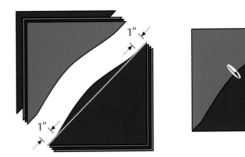

4. Repeat steps 2 and 3 with the remaining decks to make 70 blocks.

# ASSEMBLY

1. Arrange the blocks as shown below, switching the blocks around until you're satisfied with their placement. It's always fun at this stage to rotate the blocks and preview the different designs the blocks create. Do not sew the blocks together.

2. Place the light squares in the dark corners of the blocks and the dark squares in the light corners of the blocks as shown. Not every block will have a square. I tried to work the diagonal line of squares alternating between large and small squares; however, you could easily position them differently, change the size of the squares, or even use rectangles.

3. Once you're satisfied with the arrangement, work with one block at a time and then replace it in the layout. Use a chalk marker and draw a line as shown below. For a 3" square, mark a line 2½" from the edge of the block. For a 4" square, mark a line 3½" from the edge of the block. If you change the size of the squares or want to add rectangles instead, the magic number to measure from the edge is ½" less than the width of the added piece.

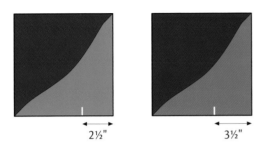

2½"     3½"

4. Place the square on the block, right sides together, with the right edge of the square aligned with the chalk line as shown. Starting ¼" from the top, use a ¼" seam allowance to sew along the right edge of the square.

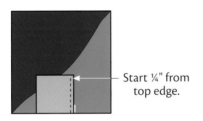

Start ¼" from top edge.

5. Finger-press ¼" of the top raw edge of the square down, then flip the square over, covering the seam allowance.

6. Use matching thread and topstitch ⅛" from the top folded edge of the square. Press the block. I like to trim the excess fabric from under the added square, but this isn't essential. Continue using this method to complete all the blocks with the added squares, replacing them in the layout as you go.

7. Pin and sew the blocks into 10 horizontal rows of seven blocks each. Press the seam allowances from row to row in opposing directions.

8. Pin and sew the rows together. Press seam allowances in one direction.

## FINISHING

Refer to "Finishing the Quilt" on page 9 as needed.

1. Divide the backing fabric crosswise into two equal panels, each approximately 60" long. Remove the selvages and sew the pieces together along a long edge to make a backing piece approximately 59" x 80"; press the seam allowances to one side.

2. Layer the quilt top with the batting and backing, keeping the backing seam parallel to the short edges of the quilt top. Baste the layers together using your favorite method.

3. Hand or machine quilt as desired. My quilt was long-arm quilted with a medium-sized stipple pattern.

4. Trim the backing and batting even with the edges of the quilt top and use the 2½"-wide strips to bind the quilt.

# PLAID PASSION

I have a fascination with plaid designs, so what could be more natural than to enlarge the idea into a quilt? It is hard to find the actual blocks with this quilt, and once you get the uneven sashing sewn on, you'll have your own unique plaid creation.

## MATERIALS

*All yardages are based on 42"-wide fabric.*

⅜ yard *each* of 3 different jewel-tone fuchsia prints for blocks

⅜ yard *each* of 3 different dark red prints for blocks

⅜ yard *each* of 3 different bright red prints for blocks

⅜ yard *each* of 2 different black prints with white for blocks

½ yard *each* of 2 different white prints with black for blocks

½ yard *each* of 2 different black prints with white for sashing (can be the same as block fabrics if desired)

⅝ yard of binding fabric

3½ yards of backing fabric

60" x 80" piece of batting

## fabric tips

I chose vivid red and pink prints that appear as a solid from a distance and that have just enough movement to make the blocks interesting. I can't stress enough the value of standing back and using my "10-foot rule" (page 5) for evaluating how the fabrics work together. It's easy to choose reds that look different from one another at close range, but once they're stitched together in the block they may all read the same. I suggest layering the fabrics side by side on a design wall or across the back of a chair. Stand back and take a look to make sure there really is a visual difference in the prints.

Finished Quilt: 50" x 70"  •  Finished Block: 35 blocks, 9" x 9"
Pieced and quilted by Karla Alexander

# CUTTING

*All measurements include ¼" seam allowances.*

**From each of the red and fuchsia prints for blocks, cut:**
1 strip, 9" x 42"; cut into 4 squares, 9" x 9" (36 total, 1 will be unused)

**From one of the black prints with white for blocks, cut:**
9 strips, 1" x 42"; cut into 35 rectangles, 1" x 9". Label these "A."

**From the other black print with white for blocks, cut:**
9 strips, 1" x 42", cut into 35 rectangles, 1" x 9". Label these "B."

**From one of the white prints with black for blocks, cut:**
9 strips, 1½" x 42"; cut into 35 rectangles, 1½" x 9". Label these "C."

**From the other white print with black for blocks, cut:**
9 strips, 1½" x 42"; cut into 35 rectangles, 1½" x 9½". Label these "D."

**From one of the black prints with white for sashing, cut:**
5 strips, 1½" x 42"; cut into 20 rectangles, 1½" x 9½"

2 strips, 1½" x 42"; cut into 4 strips, 1½" x 19½"

2 strips, 1½" x 42"; cut into 2 strips, 1½" x 29½"

**From the other black print with white for sashing, cut:**
3 strips, 2" x 42"; cut into:

    2 strips, 2" x 29½"

    4 rectangles, 2" x 9½"

4 strips, 2" x 42"

**From the binding fabric, cut:**
7 strips, 2½" x 42"

# MAKING THE BLOCKS

Refer to "Stack the Deck Blocks" on page 6 as needed.

1.  Arrange the assorted red and fuchsia squares right side up into seven decks of five squares each. Each deck should contain a different mix of fabrics. Secure each stack with a pin through all the layers.

2.  Work with one deck at a time and make sure the edges are all perfectly aligned before cutting. Measure and cut the deck vertically 7" from the right edge. Peel the top fabric off of the right stack and shuffle it to the bottom of that stack.

3.  Starting with the two fabrics on top of the stacks, pin and sew an A rectangle between the right and left portions, aligning edges and being careful to use an accurate ¼" seam allowance. Press the seam allowances toward the A rectangle. Repeat for the remaining layers and restack, keeping the blocks in the exact order they were in after step 2.

Shuffle 1 fabric from right stack.

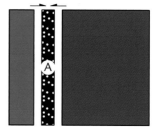

## karla's tip

Pretreat each square as well as the sashing strips with your favorite sizing spray before cutting. Use the sizing as necessary as you sew to help prevent block distortion.

Find your exact ¼" seam allowance before sewing to help keep your blocks square.

Once you sew the 9" rectangles to the first section of the block, pin the second section in place and open up to make sure the seams match across the rectangle. Do this each time you add a new rectangle to help keep the lines straight for the plaid appearance. When you sew a black and white rectangle to the block, make sure the seams of the other pieces align across the new rectangle. This will keep the lines straight for the plaid appearance.

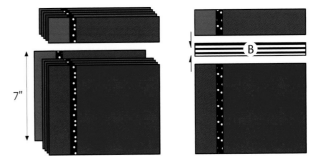

Shuffle 1 layer from lower stack.

4. For the second cut, measure and cut horizontally 7" from the bottom edge. Peel the top fabric from the lower stack and shuffle it to the bottom of that stack. It's very important to keep the blocks and layers in the same position each time you cut. After this step I always make sure the smallest piece is at the upper-left corner before I cut.

5. Starting with the top layer, pin and sew a B rectangle between the upper and lower sections, aligning edges. Press seam allowances toward the B rectangle. Repeat for the remaining layers and restack,

6. For the third cut, measure 4½" from the right edge and cut the stack vertically. *Peel the top 3 units off of the right stack and shuffle them to the bottom of that stack.*

7. Starting with the top layer, pin and sew a C rectangle between the left and right sections, aligning edges and being careful to use an accurate ¼" seam allowance. Press seam allowances toward the C rectangle. Repeat for the remaining layers, and restack the deck, keeping the blocks in the exact order and orientation they were in after step 6.

Shuffle 3 layers from right stack.

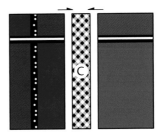

8. For the fourth cut, measure and cut horizontally 4½" from the bottom edge. Move the top unit from the lower stack and shuffle it to the bottom of that stack.

9. Starting with the top layer, pin and sew a D rectangle between the upper and lower sections, aligning edges and being careful to use an accurate ¼" seam allowance. Press seam allowances toward the D rectangle. Repeat for the remaining layers, keeping the blocks in the exact order and orientation they were in after step 8.

4½"

Shuffle 1 layer from lower stack.

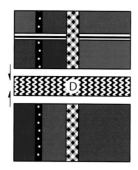

10. Repeat steps 2–9 with the remaining decks to make 35 blocks.

## ASSEMBLY

Refer to the illustration on page 45 as needed.

1. Arrange the blocks into five rows of seven blocks each, being careful to orient all the blocks in the same direction with the smallest square at the upper-left corner. Arrange the blocks so identical prints are not side by side. View your arrangement using my "10-foot rule" to check the visual balance and orientation of the blocks. Group the blocks in sections as shown.

2. Pin and sew 20 sashing rectangles, 1½" x 9½", horizontally between the blocks as shown. Press seam allowances toward the sashing.

3. Pin and sew four 1½" x 19½" sashing strips vertically in sections 1 and 2. Repeat for section three with two 1½" x 29½" sashing strips. Press seam allowances toward the sashing.

4. Pin and sew a 2" x 29½" sashing strip horizontally to join section 1 with section 2. Repeat to join section 2 with section 3. Press seam allowances toward the sashing.

5. Pin and sew a 2" x 9½" sashing rectangle horizontally to join section 4 to section 5. Repeat to join section 5 to section 6, section 7 to section 8, and section 8 to section 9. Press seam allowances toward the sashing.

6. Sew the 2" x 42" sashing strips end to end to make one long strip. Measure the quilt sections from top to bottom. (If you cut and sewed perfectly, they will measure 70½".) From the long strip, cut two sashing strips to this measurement. Pin and sew the sashing strips to join the sections. Press seam allowances toward the sashing.

# FINISHING

Refer to "Finishing the Quilt" on page 9 as needed.

1.  Divide the backing fabric crosswise into two equal panels, each approximately 60" long. Remove the selvages and sew the pieces together along a long edge to make a backing piece approximately 60" x 80"; press the seam allowances to one side.

2.  Layer the quilt top with the batting and backing, keeping the backing seam parallel to the short edges of the quilt top. Baste the layers together using your favorite method.

3.  Hand or machine quilt as desired. I machine quilted mine by stitching in the ditch to further emphasize the plaid design.

4.  Trim the backing and batting even with the edges of the quilt top and use the 2½"-wide strips to bind the quilt.

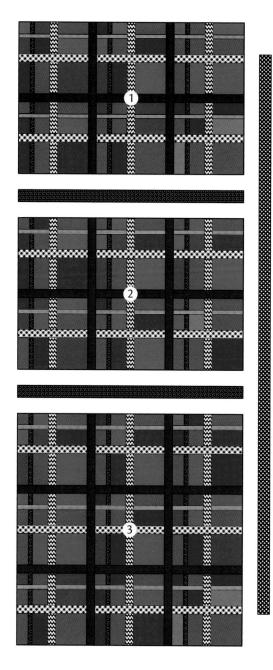
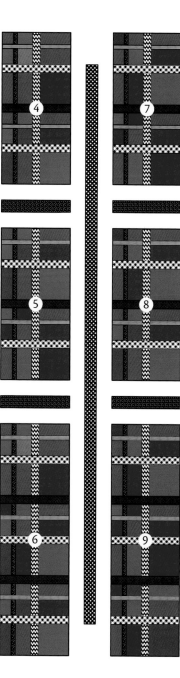

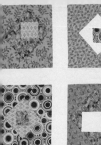

# SHAKEN Not STIRRED

A little square or rectangle appears to shake around in the center of each of the blocks in this quilt. To change things up a bit, I decided to float a few of the blocks by using a white square in the mix, resulting in several blocks that seem to melt into the sashing.

## MATERIALS

All yardages are based on 42"-wide fabric.

2⅞ yards of white fabric for blocks, sashing, and border

⅜ yard *each* of 5 different turquoise prints for blocks

⅜ yard *each* of 5 different green prints for blocks

1 square, 10½" x 10½", of dark blue (optional)

¾ yard of red print for binding

5¼ yards of backing fabric

73" x 92" piece of batting

Freezer paper (optional)

### fabric tips

For this quilt I chose colors that look clean and crisp next to one another. I used my "10-foot rule" (page 5) to pair the square colors together. Prints with tone-on-tone designs work well and don't detract from the blocks. I searched for some really lime greens as well as avocado greens. Next, bright turquoises and then a bit of medium dark blue were added to the mix. The white is actually a tone-on-tone with a slight pattern to make the blocks really pop.

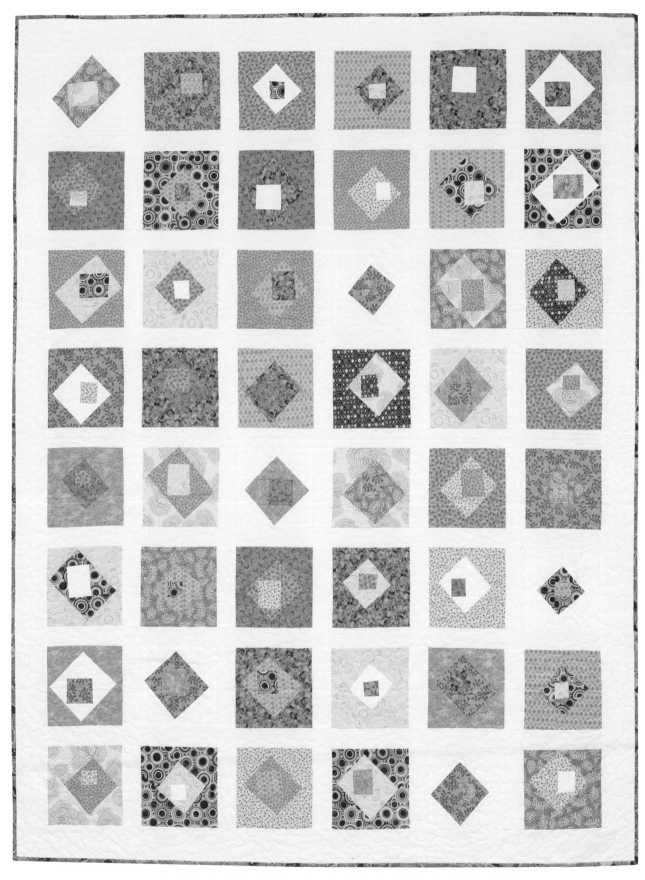

Finished Quilt: 62" x 82"   •   Finished Block: 48 blocks, 7½" x 7½"
Pieced by Karla Alexander, quilted by Dave Suderman

## CUTTING

*All measurements include ¼" seam allowances.*

From *each* of the turquoise prints, cut:

1 strip, 10½" x 42"; cut into a total of 21 squares, 10½" x 10½"

From *each* of the green prints, cut:

1 strip, 10½" x 42"; cut into a total of 21 squares, 10½" x 10½"

From the white fabric, cut:

2 strips, 10½" x 42"; cut into 6 squares, 10½" x 10½"

18 strips, 2½" x 42"; cut 8 of the strips into 40 rectangles, 2½" x 8"

7 strips, 4" x 42"

From the red print, cut:

8 strips, 2½" x 42"

## MAKING THE BLOCKS

Refer to "Stack the Deck Blocks" on page 6 as needed. The pieces are cut in two "rounds" (round 1 and round 2), which will be labeled from the center outward in the sewing order. This is the opposite of the cutting order. In the diagram at right, the round numbers are blue and the piece numbers are black.

### karla's tip

A good way to get a sneak preview of what your block will look like, without cutting a lot of fabric, is to take a solid piece of scrap fabric, 10½" x 10½", and cut as shown in the illustration at right. Sew the square back together. Check it out and see if you like the sizes and angles—this will help you determine how you want to cut your decks.

When cutting the decks, I cut each stack different from the next to create lots of variation. A fun trick for doing this is to first cut a square or rectangle out of freezer paper. The smallest width I suggest is 1½" and the

largest is 2¼". Experiment with different sizes. Use a hot, dry iron and press the square or rectangle in the center of the top layer on a deck. After cutting off the four corners (round 2), use your ruler and cut round 1 just off the edge of the paper. Keep your template if you like and next time move it a little off-center, and/or cut ¼" from one edge as desired. This gives you a little more control over where the center square ends up as well as how big it will be. Keep in mind, ¼" around each center piece will be taken up in seam allowances once the block is complete. Cut and sew only one deck at a time, so that you can change the cuts as you go.

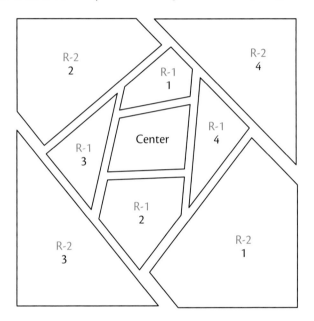

1. Arrange the 10½" x 10½" squares into eight decks of six squares each. Here's how I chose colors for my decks, but I encourage you to mix yours however you prefer:

   **3 decks:** 1 white square, 3 turquoise squares, and 2 green squares

   **3 decks:** 1 white square, 2 turquoise squares, and 3 green squares

   **1 deck:** 3 turquoise squares and 3 green squares

   **1 deck:** 1 dark blue square, 2 turquoise squares, and 3 green squares. The dark blue square is for added variation, and is purely optional. You could even shake it up with an entirely different color, such as orange or red!

   Secure each deck with a pin through all the layers until ready to sew.

2. For the first deck, use the illustration on page 48 as a guideline for the sizes and angles of your cuts. Make the first cuts, slicing the upper-right corner (piece 4) and the lower-left corner (piece 3) of the deck. Slide these stacks out of the way, and then cut the upper-left corner (piece 2) and the lower-right corner (piece 1). These four outer segments are round 2. Slide the cut segments away from the center of the deck.

3. Cut the right and left sides of the deck (round 1, pieces 4 and 3), leaving at least 1½" for the center square or rectangle. Slide the cut segments out of the way, and then cut the top and bottom edges (round 1, pieces 2 and 1), once again leaving at least 1½" for the center square or rectangle. These four inner segments will be round 1, pieces 1, 2, 3, and 4.

4. Shuffle the deck by peeling the top layer of round 1, pieces 1 through 4 off the top of the deck and placing them on the bottom of their respective stacks. Shuffle the center stack by peeling the top two fabrics and placing them on the bottom of that stack. I suggest pinning the entire deck, through all layers, to a big piece of paper before beginning to sew.

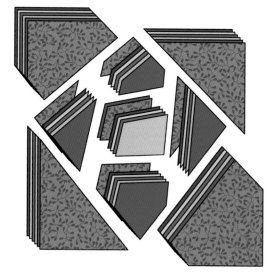

5. Chain piece round 1, pieces 1 and 2 to the center. (See "Chain Piecing" on page 7.) Press seam allowances toward the added pieces.

6. Position and chain piece round 1, pieces 3 and 4 to each center unit. Press seam allowances toward the added pieces. Return the units to the cutting mat and trim off the excess fabric so all four sides have a clean, straight edge. Stack units in the exact shuffled order.

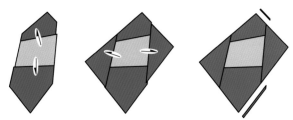

7. Add round 2, pieces 1 and 2 as shown below. The outer corners of these pieces are the corners of the block, so try to position them oriented approximately 180° from each other. Press seam allowances toward the added pieces. Return the units to the cutting mat and trim off the excess.

8. Add round 2, pieces 3 and 4. Once again, try to position the outer corners so they are exactly opposite one another. Press seam allowances toward the added pieces. Return the units to the cutting mat and trim the blocks to 8" x 8". If your blocks are a lot larger than this, you can trim to a larger size but be aware that you will need to adjust the length of the sashing strips to match. Repeat steps 1–7 to make 48 blocks.

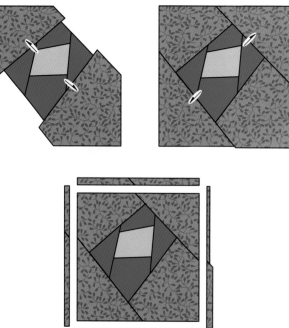

Trim to 8" x 8".

## ADDING SASHING

1. Arrange the blocks into eight horizontal rows of six blocks each. Switch and rotate the blocks around until you're satisfied with the layout. Arrange the blocks so identical prints are not side by side. View your arrangement from a distance using my "10-foot rule" to check the visual balance.

2. Sew a 2½" x 8" sashing strip vertically between each of the blocks as shown below. Press seam allowances toward the blocks. Make eight rows.

3. Sew the white 2½" x 42" strips end to end into one long length. Measure the width of a row and cut seven long sashing strips to that measurement, approximately 55½".

4. Pin and sew a long sashing strip to the bottom of every row except the bottom row. Press seam allowances toward the blocks.

5. Pin and sew the rows together in four sets of two rows each. Make sure to match the block seams from row to row across the sashing. Press seam allowances toward the blocks.

6. Pin and sew two sets of two rows together, then pin and sew the sections together. Press seam allowances toward the blocks.

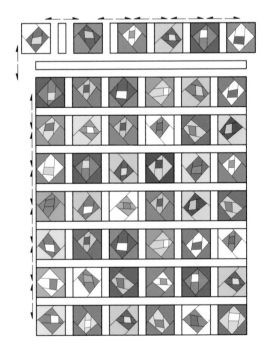

## ADDING BORDERS

Refer to "Borders" on page 9 as needed.

1. Sew the 4"-wide white strips together end to end to make one long strip.

2. Fold the long border strip in half lengthwise, matching short ends. Vertically center the folded border directly under the quilt top and trim the border strip even with the edges of the quilt top.

3. Pin and sew the borders to the sides of the quilt. Press the seam allowances toward the borders.

4. Repeat steps 2 and 3, centering the border strip horizontally under the quilt top, to cut and add the top and bottom borders.

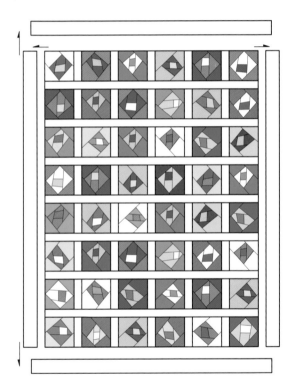

## FINISHING

Refer to "Finishing the Quilt" on page 9 as needed.

1.  Divide the backing fabric crosswise into two equal panels, each approximately 92" long. Remove the selvages and sew the pieces together along a long edge to make a backing piece approximately 73" x 92"; press the seam allowances to one side.

2.  Layer the quilt top with the batting and backing, keeping the backing seam parallel to the long edges of the quilt top. Baste the layers together using your favorite method.

3.  Hand or machine quilt as desired. My quilt was long-arm quilted with a medium-sized stipple pattern.

4.  Trim the backing and batting even with the edges of the quilt top and use the 2½"-wide strips to bind the quilt.

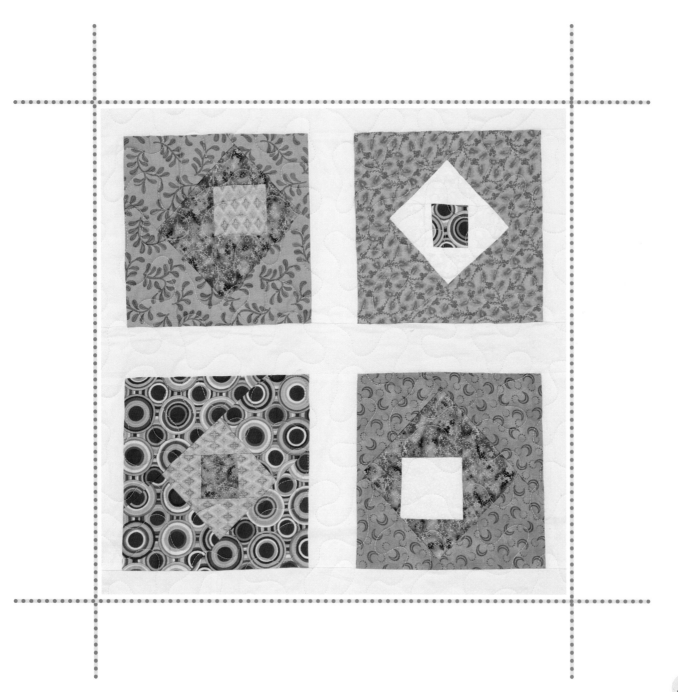

# Sideways

More than a stripe, less than a plaid, this simple strip design is perfect when you have fabrics in your favorite colors. No hurries, no worries—just let the colors mix and mingle across your quilt in a variety of lengths and widths.

## MATERIALS

*All yardages are based on 42"-wide fabric.*

⅓ yard *each* of 4 different white prints for strips

⅓ yard *each* of 4 different brown prints for strips

⅓ yard *each* of 4 different red prints for strips

⅓ yard *each* of 4 different green prints for strips

⅓ yard *each* of 4 different pink prints for strips

¾ yard of binding fabric

5½ yards of backing fabric

68" x 99" piece of batting

## fabric tips

I previewed fabric for this quilt by pinning prints side by side on my design wall and then using my "10-foot rule" (page 5) to decide what I liked. I began with the five core colors: white, brown, red, green, and pink. Then I chose variations of each color with small-scale prints and in lighter and darker values. Once again, I always backed up approximately 10 feet to take a look until I was satisfied with my choices. While many of my fabrics are tone-on-tone prints, an equal amount are small-scale prints.

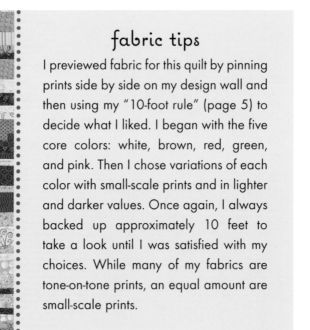

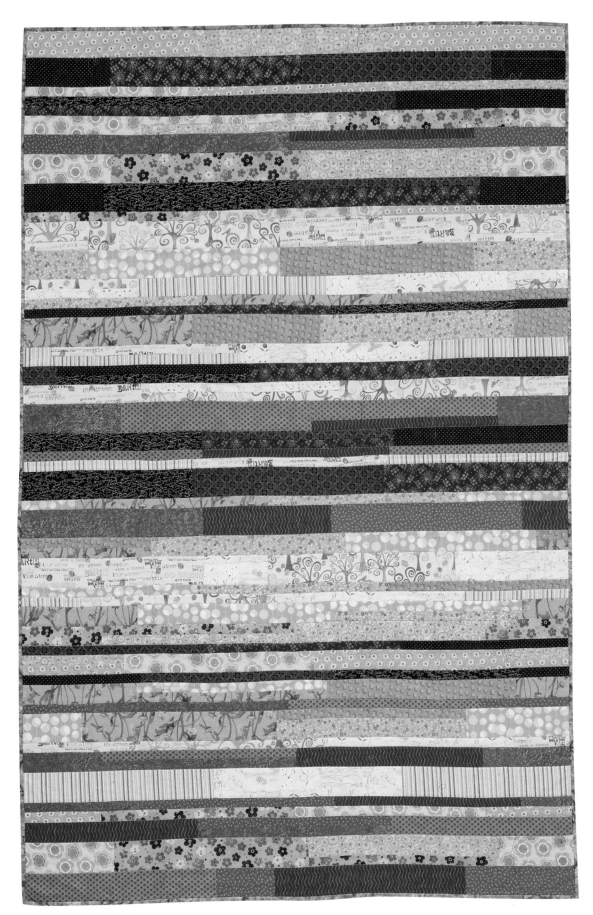

Finished Quilt: 58½" x 89"
Pieced and quilted by Karla Alexander

# CUTTING

*All measurements include ¼" seam allowances.*

**From *each* of the 20 different prints, cut:**

1 strip, 3½" x 42"; cut in half crosswise to make 2 strips approximately 20" long (40 total)

1 strip, 2½" x 42"; cut in half crosswise to make 2 strips approximately 20" long (40 total)

2 strips, 1½" x 42"; cut in half crosswise to make 4 strips approximately 20" long (80 total)

**From the binding fabric, cut:**

8 strips, 2½" x 42"

# MAKING THE STRIP ROWS

1. Trim all the selvages from the strips. Randomly choose three different 1½"-wide green strips and sew them together short end to short end to make one long strip. Make three long strip sets for each color group (15 total).

Make 3 of each color group (15 total).

2. Randomly choose two different 1½"-wide green strips. Sew the strips together along the long edges as shown below. Press the seam allowances to one side. Make three sets for each color group (15 total).

3. Randomly choose two different 2½"-wide green strips and sew them together short end to short end. Sew this strip set to the unit from step 2, short end to short end. Press seam allowances to one side. Make three sets for each color group (15 total).

Make 3 of each color group (15 total).

4. Randomly pick one 1½"-wide green strip and one 2½"-wide green strip. Sew the strips together along the long edges as shown below. Press the seam allowances to one side.

5. Randomly choose two different 3½"-wide green strips and sew them together short end to short end. Sew this strip set to the strip set from step 4, short end to short end. Press the seam allowances to one side. Make three sets for each color group (15 total).

Make 3 of each color group (15 total).

6. Randomly choose three different 3½"-wide green strips and sew them together short end to short end. Press seam allowances to one side. Make three sets for each color group (15 total).

Make 3 of each color group (15 total).

7. Randomly choose a row and slice off one end, anywhere from 5" to 10". Sew this section to the opposite end of the row. You may want to lay your quilt out and then decide where to divide the strips. Have fun with this step and randomly cut different measurements each time. I chose to cut apart and resew about half the rows until I liked the appearance.

# ASSEMBLY

1. Refer to the photograph on page 53 for suggestions on color and strip-set placement. There isn't a wrong way to do this, so enjoy and "work it" until you like how it looks. My design has 43 rows. Sometimes I placed the same prints next to each and other times I separated them. Again, work with your design until you're satisfied. You will have rows left over.

2. Trim rows 58" wide or the width of the shortest row.

3. Sew rows together in sections of four to six rows each. Because all the seams run parallel, it's easy to distort the rows and end up with arcs instead of nice, straight sections. To avoid curving rows, I did three things: first, I used spray sizing as I sewed; second, I pinned the rows together to prevent stretching; and third, I always alternated sewing directions from row to row. Sew sections together and press seam allowances in one direction.

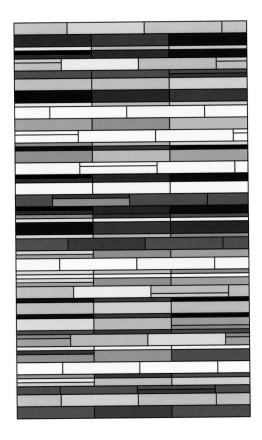

## FINISHING

Refer to "Finishing the Quilt" on page 9 as needed.

1. Divide the backing fabric crosswise into two panels, each approximately 98" long. Remove the selvages and sew the pieces together along a long edge to make a backing piece approximately 68" x 98". Press the seam allowances to one side.

2. Layer the quilt top with the batting and backing, with the backing seam parallel to the long edges of the quilt top. Baste the layers together using your favorite method.

3. Hand or machine quilt as desired. I stitched in the ditch in the horizontal rows and used a long, wavy, spiraling stipple pattern alternately placed vertically across the quilt top.

4. Trim the backing and batting even with the edges of the quilt top and use the 2½"-wide strips to bind the quilt.

# QUILTER'S WEAVE

This quilt was inspired by a tile entrance to a restaurant. I snapped a picture of it and soon found it was a familiar quilt block! The colors in the entrance were gray, brown, and a burnt red. I wanted my quilt to be a bit more snappy, so I chose a brighter palette, but I am anxious to try it someday with more subdued colors as well as a border.

## MATERIALS

*All yardages are based on 42"-wide fabric.*

½ yard *each* of 2 different light-value lime green prints for blocks

½ yard *each* of 6 different medium-value turquoise blue prints for blocks

½ yard *each* of 6 different dark purple prints for blocks

⅔ yard of binding fabric

5 yards of backing fabric

70" x 88" piece of batting

### fabric tips

I chose clear blues with strong, contrasting darker purples for the blocks and two different lighter-value lime greens for the block centers. When choosing your prints, make sure they appear different from a distance. Often, I like to throw in an additional print just to liven things up, so if you notice a larger variety of prints than what is listed, that's why!

Finished Quilt: 60" x 78"  •  Finished Block: 130 blocks, 6" x 6"
Pieced and quilted by Karla Alexander

# CUTTING

**From *each* of the 2 light-value lime green prints, cut:**

5 strips, 2½" x 42"; cut into 65 squares, 2½" x 2½" (130 squares total). Keep the two prints separate; label one green for the A blocks and the other green for the B blocks.

**From *each* of the 6 medium-value turquoise blue prints, cut:**

6 strips, 2½" x 42"; cut into 43 rectangles, 2½" x 4½" (258 rectangles total)

**From *each* of the 6 dark purple prints, cut:**

6 strips, 2½" x 42"; cut into 43 rectangles, 2½" x 4½" (258 rectangles total)

**From the binding fabric, cut:**

7 strips, 2½" x 42"

# MAKING THE BLOCKS

Make all the A blocks first. Set aside the B squares until the A blocks are complete.

1.  Randomly choose two purple and two turquoise blue rectangles. Sew a green A square to one side of a purple rectangle, aligning the top edges and using a partial seam as shown. Open the unit and finger-press the seam allowance toward the rectangle.

2.  Rotate the block 90° so that the purple rectangle is at the top. Sew a turquoise blue rectangle to the entire length of the right edge of the unit. Open the unit and finger-press the seam allowances toward the blue rectangle.

    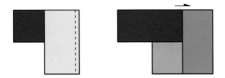

3.  Rotate the block 90° so that the turquoise blue rectangle is at the top. Sew the second purple rectangle to the right edge of the unit. Open the unit and finger-press the seam allowances toward the purple rectangle.

    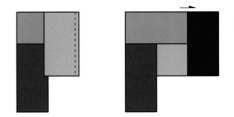

4.  Rotate the block 90° so that the purple rectangle sewn in step 3 is at the top. Sew a turquoise blue rectangle to the entire length of the right edge. (Make sure to move the first purple rectangle out of the sewing area so you don't accidentally catch it in your seam.) Open the unit and finger-press the seam allowances toward the turquoise blue rectangle.

5.  Flip the block over so that the seam allowances are facing you. Overlapping the first seam at least ¼", place the needle of your sewing machine exactly in a hole of the partial seam of the green square. Complete the seam by sewing the rest of the way along the edge of the purple rectangle. Finger-press the seam allowances toward the purple rectangle.

    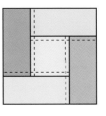

    A block.
    Make 65.

6. Repeat steps 1–5 to make 65 A blocks. Press the blocks with an iron once they are all sewn.

7. For the B blocks, repeat steps 1–6, but rotate the units and position the rectangles as described here. To begin, sew a green B square to one side of a purple rectangle, aligning the bottom edges, and using a partial seam as shown. This time you will always rotate the block so the green square is at the top before sewing the next piece. Always finger-press the seam allowances toward the green center square. Make 65 B blocks. Press the blocks with an iron once they are all sewn. The B blocks will be a mirror image of the A blocks.

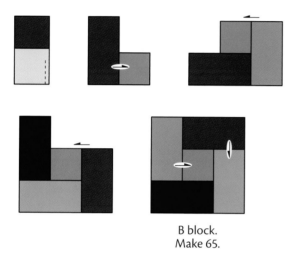

B block.
Make 65.

## ASSEMBLY

1. Arrange the blocks into 10 vertical rows of 13 blocks each. Alternate the A blocks with the B blocks, rotating them as shown so the purple rectangles are horizontal and the turquoise blue rectangles are vertical.

2. Arrange the blocks so identical prints are not side by side. View your arrangement from a distance using my "10-foot rule" (page 5) to check the visual balance.

3. Sew the blocks into 13 horizontal rows. Press seam allowances in alternating directions from row to row.

4. Sew the rows together in six sets of two each with one row left over. Combine the sets into three sets of fours rows each. Combine the sets and add the thirteenth row. Press seam allowances in one direction.

## FINISHING

Refer to "Finishing the Quilt" on page 9 as needed.

1. Divide the backing fabric crosswise into two equal panels, each approximately 88" long. Remove the selvages and sew the pieces together along a long edge to make a backing piece approximately 70" x 88"; press the seam allowances to one side.

2. Layer the quilt top with the batting and backing, keeping the backing seam parallel to the long edges of the quilt top. Baste the layers together using your favorite method.

3. Hand or machine quilt as desired. My quilt was long-arm quilted with a medium-sized stipple pattern.

4. Trim the backing and batting even with the edges of the quilt top and use the 2½"-wide strips to bind the quilt.

# Out of Line

The blocks for this quilt are easy to make using simple squares and my "stack the deck" technique. The skewed cuts create asymmetrical blocks—half appear to be squeezed in the middle while the other half have a rounded appearance.

## MATERIALS

*All yardages are based on 42"-wide fabric.*

1⅝ yards of medium-value orangish red batik for outer border

⅜ yard *each* of 8 different light-value brown and gray batiks for blocks

⅜ yard *each* of 8 different medium-dark-value orangish red batiks for blocks

⅜ yard of green batik for inner border

¾ yard of binding fabric

5½ yards of backing fabric

80" x 97" piece of batting

## fabric tips

For a softly glowing effect, I chose two contrasting groups of batiks in earth tones of burnt reds and soft browns with a touch of green and gray. To accentuate the unusual angles in the blocks, fabrics that appear as solid work best for this design.

Finished Quilt: 71" x 87"  •  Finished Block: 63 blocks, 8" x 8"
Pieced and quilted by Karla Alexander

## CUTTING

*All measurements include ¼" seam allowances.*

**From *each* of the 8 different light brown and gray batiks, cut:**

1 strip, 9" x 42"; cut each strip into 4 squares, 9" x 9" (32 total)

**From *each* of the 8 different medium-dark orangish red batiks, cut:**

1 strip, 9" x 42"; cut each strip into 4 squares, 9" x 9" (32 total)

**From the green batik, cut:**

7 strips, 1½" x 42"

**From the medium-value orangish red batik, cut from the lengthwise grain:**

6 strips, 6½" x length of fabric

**From the binding fabric, cut:**

9 strips, 2½" x 42"

## MAKING THE BLOCKS

Refer to "Stack the Deck Blocks" on page 6 as needed.

1.  Alternating light and medium-dark fabrics, arrange the 9" squares, right sides up, into 16 decks of four squares each. Each deck should contain a different mix of fabrics. Secure each deck with a pin through all the layers.

2.  Work with one deck at a time and make sure the edges are all aligned. Use a ruler to measure and cut 4" from the lower-left corner to 4" from the upper-right corner as shown. Repeat, cutting from side to side, 4" from the lower-left corner to 4" from the upper-right corner. You will have four small stacks as shown.

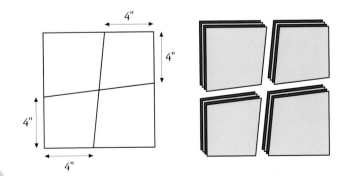

3.  Shuffle the order of the fabrics as follows: Peel the top fabric from the upper-right stack and place it on the bottom of that stack. Peel the top two fabrics from the lower-right stack and place them on the bottom of that stack. Peel the top three fabrics from the lower-left stack and place them on the bottom of that stack. Do not shuffle the upper-left stack.

4.  Sew the blocks one layer at a time. Pin the upper two pieces right sides together along the sewing edge. Check to make sure they will align along the top and bottom edges once they are sewn. Sew, and press the seam allowances to one side. Repeat for the bottom two pieces. Press the seam allowances in the opposite direction of the top unit.

5.  Pin and sew the top and bottom units together, matching the center seams. Centers will be slightly offset on the seam-allowance edges but should match on the sewing lines. Press the seam allowances in one direction. Make four blocks. You will have two A blocks with light 5"-cut corners and two B blocks with medium-dark 5"-cut corners.

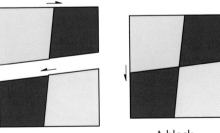

A block

B block

6. Repeat steps 2–5 to make a total of 64 blocks. Keep the blocks separated into A and B stacks.

## ASSEMBLY

1. Arrange the blocks into seven horizontal rows of nine blocks each, alternating the A and B blocks. Rotate the B blocks to form the patchwork design as shown below. Always position blocks with dark values in the upper-right side. You will have one unused block.

2. Arrange the blocks so identical prints are not side by side. When switching blocks around, remember that you must keep the A blocks in the A position and the B blocks in the B position. View your arrangement from a distance, using my "10-foot rule" (page 5) to check the visual balance.

3. Pin and sew the blocks into horizontal rows. Press seam allowances in opposite directions from row to row.

4. Pin and sew the rows together in pairs; press.

5. Pin and sew the pairs together. Clip the seam allowance ⅛" if you need to release one of the allowances so that they will alternate.

## ADDING BORDERS

Refer to "Borders" on page 9 as needed.

1. Sew the 1½"-wide green strips together end to end to make one long strip.

2. Fold the long border strip in half lengthwise, matching short ends. Vertically center the folded border directly under the quilt top. Make sure the border and the quilt top are smooth without any wrinkles or pleats. Trim the border strip even with the edges of the quilt top.

3. Pin and sew the borders to the sides of the quilt. Press the seam allowances toward the border strips.

4. Repeat steps 2 and 3, centering the folded border horizontally for the green top and bottom borders. Press seam allowances toward the borders.

5. Repeat steps 1–4 with the 6½"-wide orangish red strips to make and attach the outer border.

## FINISHING

Refer to "Finishing the Quilt" on page 9 as needed.

1. Divide the backing fabric crosswise into two equal panels, each approximately 97" long. Remove the selvages and sew the pieces together along a long edge to make a backing piece approximately 80" x 97". Press the seam allowances to one side.

2. Layer the quilt top with the batting and backing, keeping the backing seam parallel to the long edges of the quilt top. Baste the layers together using your favorite method.

3. Hand or machine quilt as desired. I machine quilted my quilt with a straight stitch, ⅜" inside each of the seams.

4. Trim the backing and batting even with the edges of the quilt top and use the 2½"-wide strips to bind the quilt.

# ELECTRIC FENCE

Okay—I admit it. Sometimes sparks do fly from my quilted imagination, and this asymmetrical tribute to summer is intended to evoke your own personal images! These bright colors scream summer fun and ocean surfing and, well, it kind of does looks like a bunch of surfboards laid out in an uneven line along a sandy beach—or maybe psychedelic fences. However you see it or dream it, it's a bright, sunny quilt with asymmetrical blocks and borders for the asymmetrical quilter. As a variation, try a symmetrical border or no border at all.

## MATERIALS

*All yardages are based on 42"-wide fabric.*

1 yard of dark blue fabric for border

½ yard *each* of 6 pink and orange prints for block end caps

⅜ yard *each* of 3 different green prints for blocks

⅜ yard *each* of 3 different blue prints for blocks

⅜ yard *each* of 3 different medium dark fuchsia and red prints for blocks

⅜ yard *each* of 3 different brown and gold prints for blocks

⅝ yard of binding fabric

4¾ yards of backing fabric

60" x 83" piece of batting

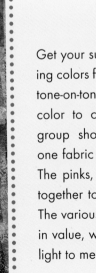

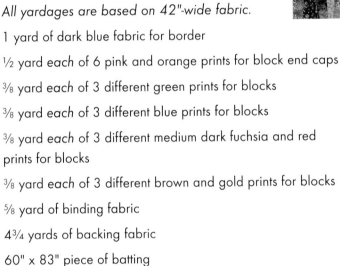

### fabric tips

Get your sunglasses on and have fun choosing colors for this quilt! To begin with, choose tone-on-tone batiks with good contrast from color to color. The fabrics in each color group should read well together without one fabric sticking out more than the others. The pinks, oranges, and reds all work well together to provide a textured appearance. The various blues are mostly medium to dark in value, while the greens lean more toward light to medium values.

Finished Quilt: 48½" x 69½"  •  Finished Block: 35 blocks, 8" x 9"
Pieced by Karla Alexander, quilted by Dave Suderman

# CUTTING

*All measurements include ¼" seam allowances.*

**From *each* of the 12 assorted green, blue, fuchsia, red, brown, and gold prints, cut:**

2 rectangles, 5½" x 11" (24 total; you will use only 23)

1 rectangle, 7½" x 11" (12 total)

**From *each* of the 6 pink and orange prints, cut:**

2 strips, 1¼" x 42"; cut each print into 4 rectangles, 1¼ x 11" (24 total; you will use only 23)

2 strips, 1¾" x 42"; cut each print into 4 rectangles, 1¾" x 11" (24 total; you will use only 23)

2 strips, 2½" x 42"; cut each print into 6 rectangles, 2½" x 7½" (36 total; you will use only 35)

2 strips, 1½" x 42"; cut each print into 6 rectangles, 1½" x 9½" (36 total; you will use only 35)

**From the dark blue fabric, cut:**

1 strip, 3" x 42"; cut into 3 rectangles, 3" x 9½"

2 strips, 2" x 42"; cut into:

   3 rectangles, 2" x 8½"

   4 rectangles, 2" x 9½"

2 strips, 1½" x 42"; cut into:

   2 rectangles, 1½" x 8½"

   4 rectangles, 1½" x 9½"

3 strips, 3" x 42"

3 strips, 4" x 42"

**From the binding fabric, cut:**

7 strips, 2½" x 42"

## MAKING THE BLOCKS

Refer to "Stack the Deck Blocks" on page 6 as needed.

1. Randomly choose and sew a 1¼" x 11" rectangle to the top long edge of each 5½" x 11" rectangle. Press seam allowances toward the 5½"-wide rectangles.

2. Randomly choose and sew a 1¾" x 11" strip to the bottom long edge of each unit from step 1. Press seam allowances toward the 5½"-wide rectangles.

3. Arrange the 23 units from step 2 with the 7½" x 11" rectangles into five decks of six layers each and one deck of five layers (6 total decks). In each deck choose a variety of pieced units mixed with the two unpieced rectangles. Layer some of the pieced units with the wide pink or orange rectangle positioned at the top and the remaining with the thin pink or orange rectangle at the top. Alternate the unpieced rectangles with the pieced units. Each deck should be very different from the next.

4. Work with one deck at a time. This way you can examine your cuts and determine how you want to cut the next deck. Cut each deck into eight sections. Make the first and last cut the widest, as more of this width will get trimmed off when constructing the block. Cut each deck differently, choosing a variation of gentle curves and straight-line cuts. Refer to "Curves" on page 8 as needed.

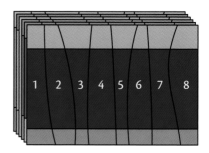

5. Shuffle the deck as follows: sections 1 and 7, shuffle one unit; sections 2 and 8, shuffle two units; section 3, shuffle three units; section 4, shuffle four units; section 5, shuffle five units; section 6, do not shuffle. Each deck will have a duplication of two different segments after shuffling. The deck with five layers will have three duplications.

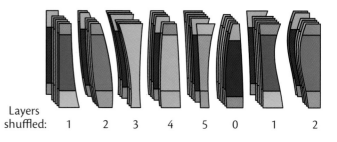

Layers shuffled:   1   2   3   4   5   0   1   2

6. Chain piece all six layers of section 1 to section 2. (See "Chain Piecing" on page 7.) You won't be sewing over another seam, so you won't need to cut the threads or stop and press.

7. Pull the sewn sections toward you and open them up one at a time. Starting with the top fabric, sew section 3 to the first combined 1/2 unit, chain piecing as before. Continue until all eight sections have been added to make six blocks. Cut threads between the blocks and press the seam allowances in one direction. Trim the blocks, if necessary, to 7½" x 7½".

8. Randomly choose and sew a pink or orange 2½" x 7½" rectangle to the bottom of each of the 35 blocks. Press the seam allowances toward the rectangle.

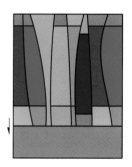

9. Randomly choose 17 blocks and label this set "block A." Label the remaining set of 18 blocks "block B." Randomly choose and sew a pink or orange 1½" x 9½" rectangle to the right side of block A and to the left side of block B.

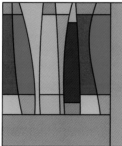

Block A.
Make 17.

Block B.
Make 18.

## ASSEMBLY

1. Arrange the 35 blocks into seven horizontal rows of five blocks each, alternating block A with block B as shown below. Note that in the first row, block A and block B are rotated so the narrow pink or orange strip is positioned on the left. Rotate the A and B blocks 180° from row to row.

2. Add the dark blue rectangles to the blocks and rows as shown. Trim the bottom edges of the two top-row blocks with the additional rectangles so the blocks measures 9½" in height to match the other blocks. Trim the top edges of the three bottom-row blocks with the additional rectangles so the blocks measure 9½" in height. (Optional: Fabric requirements are sufficient for a 5" border all the way around instead of an asymmetrical border. For this approach, cut six border strips, 5½" x 42", and refer to "Borders" on page 9 as needed.)

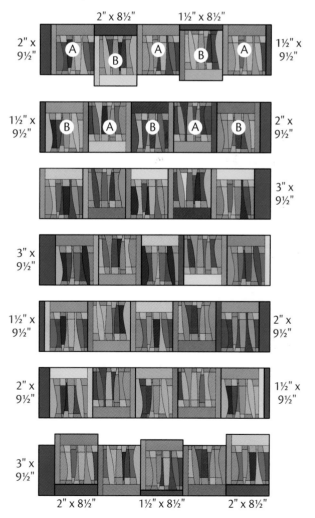

3. Pin and sew the rows together in sets of two each with one left over. Press seam allowances in opposite directions from row to row. Pin and sew the sets and the row together. Press the seam allowances to one side.

4. Remove the selvages and sew the 3"-wide blue strips together end to end to make one long, continuous strip. Press the seam allowances to one side. Repeat with the 4"-wide blue strips.

5. Measure the length of the quilt top through the center. Cut one 3"-wide border for the left side and one 4"-wide border for the right side to this measurement. Pin and sew the borders in place. Press the seam allowances toward the borders.

6. Measure the width of the quilt top through the center, including the borders just added. Cut one 3"-wide border for the top edge and one 4"-wide border for the bottom edge to this measurement. Pin and sew the borders in place. Press the seam allowances toward the borders.

## FINISHING

Refer to "Finishing the Quilt" on page 9 as needed.

1. Divide the backing fabric crosswise into two equal panels, each approximately 83" long. Remove the selvages and sew the pieces together along a long edge to make a backing piece approximately 60" x 83"; press the seam allowances to one side.

2. Layer the quilt top with the batting and backing, keeping the backing seam parallel to the long edges of the quilt top. Baste the layers together using your favorite method.

3. Hand or machine quilt as desired. My quilt was long-arm quilted with a medium-sized stipple pattern.

4. Trim the backing and batting even with the edges of the quilt top and use the 2½"-wide strips to bind the quilt.

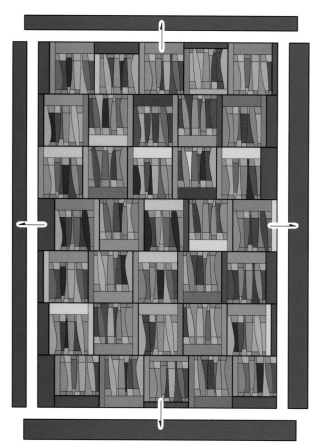

# SERENGETI

A mix of subtle-design batiks creates a flowing patchwork of soft brown and beige colors in this quilt. Through the use of my "stack the deck" methods along with cutting slightly free-form curves, each block in this awesome quilt is different from the next. If you're uncomfortable sewing curves, why not start off with very gentle curves? Or, simply make straight cuts instead.

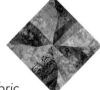

## MATERIALS

*All yardages are based on 42"-wide fabric.*

1 yard *each* of 3 different light, soft beige batiks for blocks and setting triangles

⅔ yard *each* of 2 different light, soft beige batiks for blocks

1 yard *each* of 3 different medium to dark brown batiks for blocks and setting triangles

⅔ yard *each* of 2 different medium to dark brown batiks for blocks

⅔ yard of binding fabric

5½ yards of backing fabric

72" x 97" piece of batting

## fabric tips

I like to use my "10-foot rule" (page 5) to choose the batiks for this quilt. Select subtle batiks with small- to medium-scale patterns to make sure the fabric doesn't overwhelm the block design. I tried to make sure each set of colors would distinctly read as either a medium to dark brown or a light, soft beige. Arrange the fabrics side by side and then stand back and take a look. You should be able to see a difference in the value of the brown and beige prints. I also let a few of the prints in this quilt be what I call a "player"—meaning they would look OK in either the brown or beige selection. I don't hesitate to use them, but I try to keep an equal amount of "players" in each color group.

Finished Quilt: 62½" x 87½"  •  Finished Block: 59 blocks, 8¾" x 8¾"
Pieced by Karla Alexander, quilted by Dave Suderman

# CUTTING

*All measurements include ¼" seam allowances.*

**From *each* of 3 different beige batiks for blocks and setting triangles, cut:**

2 strips, 10½" x 42"; cut each strip into 3 rectangles, 10½" x 12½" (18 total)

1 strip, 7" x 42"

**From *each* of 2 different beige batiks for blocks, cut:**

2 strips, 10½" x 42"; cut each strip into 3 rectangles, 10½" x 12½" (12 total)

**From *each* of 3 different brown batiks for blocks and setting triangles, cut:**

2 strips, 10½" x 42"; cut each strip into 3 rectangles, 10½" x 12½" (18 total)

1 strip, 7" x 42"

**From *each* of 2 different brown batiks for blocks, cut:**

2 strips, 10½" x 42"; cut each strip into 3 rectangles, 10½" x 12½" (12 total)

**From the binding fabric, cut:**

8 strips, 2½" x 42"

# MAKING THE BLOCKS

Refer to "Stack the Deck Blocks" on page 6 as needed.

1.  Arrange the 30 beige 10½" x 12½" rectangles into six decks of five rectangles each. Each deck should contain five different fabrics. Secure the decks with a pin through all layers until you're ready to sew.

2.  Work with one deck at a time. Referring to the illustration, make four skewed cuts as shown. Make the first and last cuts the widest, as more of this width will get trimmed when constructing the block. (I suggest you cut these no narrower than 1¾".)

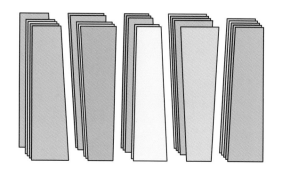

3.  Shuffle the deck by peeling the top fabric off section 1 and sliding it to the bottom of that stack. Peel the top two fabrics from section 2 and slide them to the bottom of that stack. Peel the top three fabrics from section 3 and slide them to the bottom of that stack. Peel the top four fabrics from section 4 and slide them to the bottom of that stack. Leave section 5 unshuffled. Pin the stacks to a piece of paper in the exact order they were cut and shuffled.

4.  Chain piece all five layers of section 1 to section 2. (See "Chain Piecing" on page 7.) You won't be sewing over another seam, so you won't need to cut the threads or stop and press.

5.  Pull the sewn sections toward you and open them up one at a time. Starting with the top fabric, sew section 3 to the first combined 1/2 unit, chain piecing as before. Continue until all five sections have been added to make five blocks. Cut threads between the blocks and press the seam allowances in one direction.

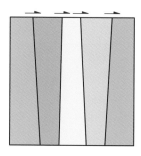

6.  Repeat steps 2–5 to make 30 beige blocks. With each deck, change the angles and width of the cuts.

7.  Repeat steps 1–6 with the brown rectangles to make 30 brown blocks.

8. Trim all the blocks to 9¾" x 9¾".

9. Arrange your finished blocks right side up in 30 decks of two blocks each, one beige and one brown. Position the beige block on the bottom with the seams horizontal. Layer a brown block on top of the beige block with the seams vertical. Match the edges as neatly as you can.

10. Working with one deck at a time, use a chalk marker to mark the top block diagonally from corner to corner in one direction. Use your ruler to cut the first inch straight, exactly on the chalk line, and then release the pressure on your ruler and let it glide along with your rotary cutter to cut a gentle curve through the middle portion of the blocks. (See "Curves" on page 8.) Straighten out the curve and cut exactly on the chalk line for the last inch.

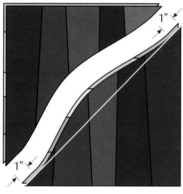

Cut first and last inch straight.

11. Shuffle the top section of the brown block under the beige section. Sew the sections together. Press the seam allowances toward the brown section.

12. Repeat steps 10 and 11 with the remaining decks to make 60 blocks. (You will use only 59.)

## MAKING THE SETTING TRIANGLES

1. Use the 45° line on your ruler and cut each of the beige and brown 7" strips into four triangles that measure 14" along their long edges, as shown. You will have enough fabric to cut 24 triangles, but you will need only 10 beige triangles and 10 brown triangles.

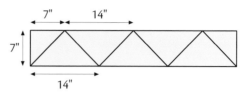

2. Set six beige and six brown triangles aside. Arrange the remaining triangles right side up into four decks of two triangles each, one beige and one brown, with the brown triangle on the top of the stack.

3. Use a chalk marker to draw a straight line through the center of the brown triangle up through the tip. Use your ruler to cut the first inch straight, exactly on the chalk line, and then release the pressure on your ruler and let it glide along with your rotary cutter to cut a gentle curve through the middle portion of the triangle. Straighten out the curve and cut exactly along the chalk line for the last inch.

4. Shuffle the top brown fabric in the stack on the left, placing it under the beige piece, and sew the sections together. Press the seam allowances toward the brown fabric. Repeat to make eight pieced setting triangles.

5. Cut two squares, 9" x 9", from any of the leftover batiks. Cut once diagonally through the center of each square to yield a total of four triangles. These triangles will be for the quilt corners and can each be cut from different fabrics if you like.

## ASSEMBLY

1. Arrange the blocks as shown, alternating the position of the brown and beige sections. Arrange the pieced setting triangles along the top and bottom edges of the quilt-block layout. Arrange the remaining triangles along the right and left sides. Add the corner setting triangles last.

2. Move the blocks around until you're satisfied with the arrangement. It's always fun at this stage to rotate the blocks and preview the different designs they create.

3. Sew the blocks and side triangles together in diagonal rows and press the seam allowances in opposing directions from row to row. Add the corner setting triangles and press the seam allowances toward the corner triangles.

Note that the corner and setting triangles are slightly oversized to allow for trimming and squaring the quilt top. For nice, straight edges, I like to trim the quilt after quilting.

## FINISHING

Refer to "Finishing the Quilt" on page 9 as needed.

1. Divide the backing fabric crosswise into two equal panels, each approximately 96" long. Remove the selvages and sew the pieces together along a long edge to make a backing piece approximately 72" x 96"; press the seam allowances to one side.

2. Layer the quilt top with the batting and backing, keeping the backing seam parallel to the long edges of the quilt top. Baste the layers together using your favorite method.

3. Hand or machine quilt as desired. My quilt was long-arm quilted with a medium-sized stipple pattern.

4. Trim the excess backing and batting by lining up the 45° measurement on your ruler along the seam line of the blocks. Measure approximately ½" beyond the outer tip of each block and trim.

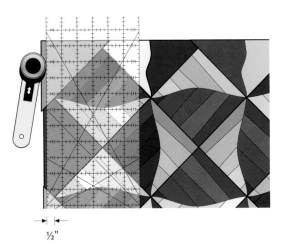

½"

5. Use the 2½"-wide strips to bind the quilt.

# PATCHWORK WAVE

I like blocks that are easy to make yet interesting enough to keep one wondering how on earth they were put together. The blocks in "Patchwork Wave" fit this description perfectly—the curves captivate the eye, but the blocks are actually simple enough to make because they have just one wavy edge. I chose two different color groups, pink and green, and then spiced it up by using six different prints in each group.

## MATERIALS

*All yardages are based on 42"-wide fabric.*

³⁄₈ yard *each* of 6 different pink prints for blocks

³⁄₈ yard *each* 6 different green prints for blocks

⁵⁄₈ yard of binding fabric

3⁵⁄₈ yards of backing fabric

63" x 80" piece of batting

### fabric tips

Any contrasting group of fabrics in two colorways will work with this design. Choose your two favorite colors and then preview how they look together by viewing them from a distance. Make sure your two colors provide enough contrast so that you'll be able to see the lines of the patchwork.

If you'd like to make a smaller or larger quilt than what's shown here, it's easy to do: the number of fabric squares you begin with equals the number of blocks you finish with.

Finished Quilt: 52½" x 70" untrimmed, 48" x 65½" trimmed  •  Finished Block: 48 blocks, 8¾" x 8¾"
Pieced by Karla Alexander, quilted by Dave Suderman

## CUTTING

*All measurements include ¼" seam allowances.*

**From *each* of the 6 different pink prints, cut:**
1 strip, 10" x 42"; cut each strip into 4 squares,
  10" x 10" (24 total)

**From *each* of the 6 different green prints, cut:**
1 strip, 10" x 42"; cut each strip into 4 squares,
  10" x 10" (24 total)

**From the binding fabric, cut:**
7 strips, 2½" x 42"

## MAKING THE BLOCKS

Refer to "Stack the Deck Blocks" on page 6 as
needed. Use your favorite sizing spray to help prevent
distortion.

1. Right sides up, and alternating the pink and green,
   arrange and neatly stack the 10" squares into 12
   decks of 4 squares each. Each deck should have a
   green fabric on the top. Secure each deck with a
   pin through all the layers.

2. Use a ruler and a chalk marker to measure and
   mark a vertical line 5" from the sides of the deck as
   shown below. Make a second chalk line horizontally, 5" from the top and bottom edges of the deck.

3. Place your ruler on the vertical chalk line. Use it to
   cut the first inch straight, exactly on the line, and
   then release the pressure on your ruler and let it
   glide along with your rotary cutter to cut a gentle
   curve through the middle portion of the deck.
   Straighten out the curve and cut exactly on the
   chalk line for the last inch.

4. Repeat step 3, this time cutting horizontally through
   the deck and crossing the vertical cut at a 90°
   angle.

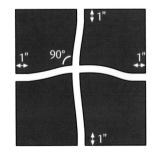

Cut first and last inches straight.
Intersect at 90°.

5. Begin shuffling the deck by peeling the top fabric
   from the upper-right stack and moving it to the
   bottom of that stack. Peel the top two fabrics from
   the lower-right stack and move them to the bottom
   of that stack. Peel the top three fabrics from the
   lower-left stack and move them to the bottom of
   that stack. Do not shuffle the fabrics in the upper-
   left stack.

6. Sew the blocks one layer at a time. Right sides
   together, pin the upper two segments along the
   sewing edge. Check the segments to make sure
   they will be even along the top and bottom edges
   once they are sewn. Stitch. Press the seam allowances in one direction.

7. Repeat step 6 with the lower two segments. Press
   the seam allowances in the opposite direction of
   the top unit.

8. Pin and sew the upper and lower units together,
   matching the center seams. Press the seam allowances in one direction. Make a total of 48 blocks.

## ASSEMBLY

1. Arrange the blocks into eight horizontal rows of six blocks each. Rotate the blocks so that the same color comes together to form single-color four patches.

2. Adjust your block placement as necessary to make sure identical prints are not side by side, and then view your arrangement from a distance using my "10-foot rule" (page 5) to check the visual balance.

3. Pin and sew the blocks into horizontal rows. Press seam allowances in alternating directions from row to row.

4. Pin and sew the rows together in pairs. Clip the seam allowance ⅛" if you need to release one of the allowances so they will alternate. Pin and sew the pairs together. Press the seam allowances in one direction.

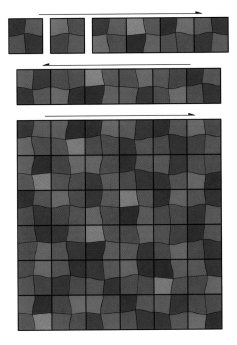

## FINISHING

Refer to "Finishing the Quilt" on page 9 as needed.

1. Divide the backing fabric crosswise into two equal panels, each approximately 63" long. Remove the selvages and sew the pieces along a long edge to make a backing piece approximately 63" x 80"; press the seam allowances to one side.

2. Layer the quilt top with the batting and backing, keeping the backing seam parallel to the short edges of the quilt top. Baste the layers together using your favorite method.

3. Hand or machine quilt as desired. My quilt was long-arm quilted with a medium-sized stipple pattern.

4. Before binding my quilt, I trimmed a 2¼"-wide strip off all four edges to create an interesting patchwork border. This is optional, of course; the backing and batting can be trimmed even with the edges of the quilt top as well.

Trim 2¼".

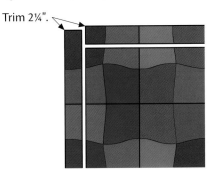

5. Use the 2½"-wide strips to bind the quilt.

# LONG CABIN

I think of the Log Cabin as a timeless quilt-block design that can take on many different looks by the use of different fabrics and different layouts. For my "Long" version, I stretched the blocks into rectangles and used a mix of different-sized logs and block centers. I like to work with one deck at a time rather than precutting all the logs a specific size. I can cut different log widths as I go, creating center rectangles or squares of all different sizes. That way, no two blocks are exactly the same.

## MATERIALS

*All yardages are based on 42"-wide fabric.*

⅜ yard *each* of 7 different pink prints for blocks

⅜ yard *each* of 8 different brown prints for blocks

⅜ yard *each* of 4 different white prints for blocks

⅜ yard *each* of 4 different green prints for blocks

½ yard of green checked fabric for inner border

1 yard of pink polka-dot fabric for outer border

⅔ yard of binding fabric

5 yards of backing fabric

71" x 90" piece of batting

## fabric tips

Choose a group of small- to medium-scale prints in a family of colors that appeals to you. I had a lot of fun mixing polka dots, plaids, stripes, and even a few floral prints. Group your choices together by lights and darks to make sure there is contrast from group to group. A fabric that might look like a dark next to one fabric might look like a light or medium next to another, so select your fabrics one block at a time. Experiment and stretch out of your comfort box! The given fabric requirements can always be added to; I have listed the necessary amounts in the instructions, but I must say that as I work my quilts, I add in fabrics as I see fit. Keep in mind, if you'd like to pull from your stash, you simply need rectangles that measure 10½" x 12". You can use the same print just once, or three or four times. Enjoy and work your colors as you go.

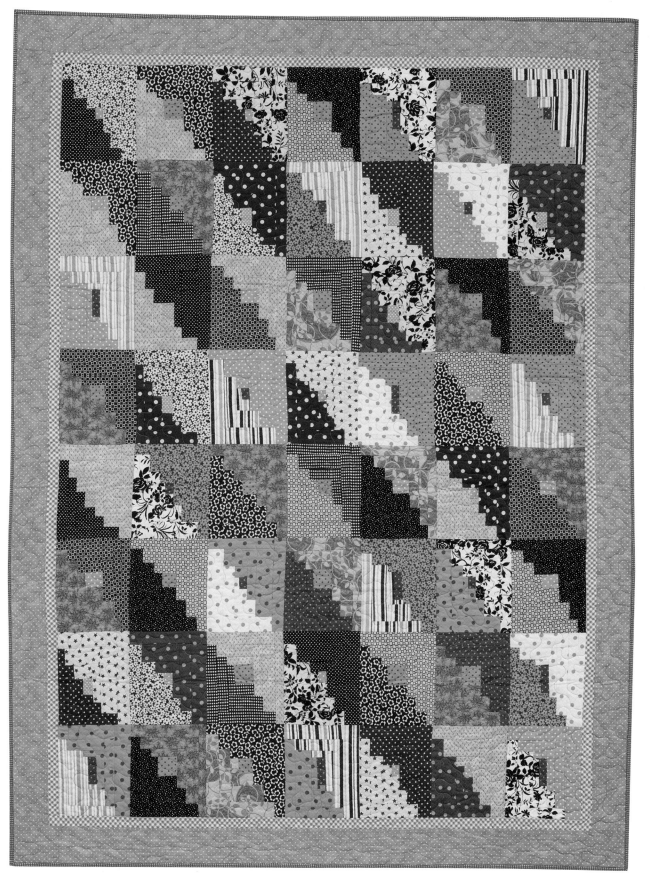

Finished Quilt: 60" x 79" • Finished Block: 56 blocks, 7" x 8½"
Pieced by Karla Alexander, quilted by Dave Suderman

# CUTTING

*All measurements include ¼" seam allowances.*

**From *each* of the pink prints, cut:**
2 or 3 rectangles, 10½" x 12", to yield 20 total

**From *each* of the brown prints, cut:**
2 or 3 rectangles, 10½" x 12", to yield 20 total

**From *each* of the white prints, cut:**
2 rectangles, 10½" x 12" (8 total)

**From *each* of the green prints, cut:**
2 rectangles, 10½" x 12" (8 total)

**From the green checked fabric, cut:**
7 strips, 2" x 42"

**From the pink polka-dot fabric, cut:**
7 strips, 4½" x 42"

**From the binding fabric, cut:**
8 strips, 2½" x 42"

# CUTTING THE BLOCKS

Refer to "Stack the Deck Blocks" on page 6 as needed.

The logs are cut in three "rounds" (rounds 1, 2, and 3), which will be labeled from the center outward in the sewing order. This is the opposite of the cutting order. In the diagram below, the round numbers are blue and the piece numbers are black. To create a different-sized center for every deck of blocks, experiment with cutting different widths. A fun way to do this is to take a 10½" x 12" piece of scrap fabric, cut it into logs of different widths, and then refer to the cutting order below and sew the square back together. The main objective is to end up with a center that isn't smaller than ½" in either direction.

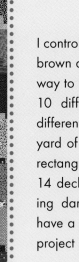

## karla's tip

I controlled the colors, grouping pink with brown and green with white, but another way to make the quilt is to simply choose 10 different light-value prints and 10 different dark-value prints. You'll need ⅜ yard of each. Cut 28 dark and 28 light rectangles, 10½" x 12", and stack into 14 decks of 4 rectangles each, alternating dark with light. Each deck should have a different mix of fabric. Follow the project instructions for making the quilt.

1. Arrange the pink and brown 10½" x 12" rectangles, right sides up, into 10 decks of four rectangles each, alternating pink and brown. Arrange the white and green 10½" x 12" rectangles, right sides up, into 4 decks of four rectangles each, alternating white and green. Each deck should have a different mix of fabric. Secure each deck with a pin through all the layers.

2. Work with one deck at a time. Cut the outermost round (round 3), starting with log 4, slicing from the right side of the deck. Slide the log out of the way and then cut log 3 across the top of the deck. Repeat for log 2 on the left side and log 1 on the bottom. Each log may be cut a different width. The logs on the sides of the blocks should be cut no narrower than ⅞" and no wider than 2". For the top and bottom logs, the cut width should be no less than 1" and no wider than 2". I suggest the following measurements in any order: for the sides, 1¾", 1½", and 1¼"; for the top and bottom logs, 2", 1½", and 1".

3. Repeat step 2 two more times, once for round 2, logs 1, 2, 3, and 4, and once for round 1, logs 1, 2, 3, and 4.

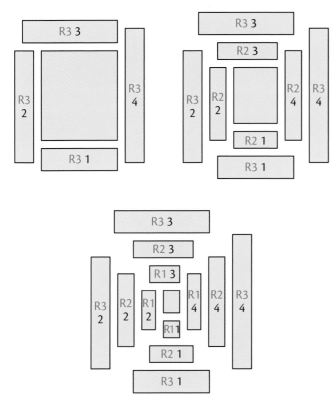

4. Use the leftover fabric from cutting the 10½" x 12" rectangles to make new centers for your blocks out of different fabrics than what is already in the stack. Lift the center stack out of the deck and use one of the pieces as a template to cut four new centers to that exact measurement. Stack the new centers and place them in the deck, being careful to orient the stack correctly.

## MAKING THE BLOCKS

1. Work with one deck at a time. Shuffle the deck by moving the top fabric from logs 1 and 2 in rounds 1, 2, and 3 to the bottom of their respective stacks. Do not shuffle logs 3 and 4.

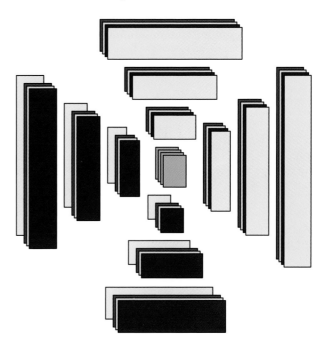

2. Chain piece all four round 1, log 1 rectangles to the center pieces as shown below. (See "Chain Piecing" on page 7.) Press seam allowances toward log 1 and restack the units in the same order they were in step 1.

3. If you're trimming the logs as you sew, measure the height of the unit from step 2. Trim the round 1, log 2 pieces to this length. Chain piece all four round 1, log 2 rectangles to the center unit as shown. Press seam allowances toward log 2 and restack the units in the same order they were in step 1.

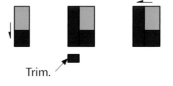

Trim.

## method for pretrimming

One of the steps in constructing a block is to trim the length of some of the logs. If you have an exact ¼" seam allowance, you can trim all your logs to size before you start to sew, following the measurements given below. If you don't have an exact ¼" seam allowance, I suggest you measure and trim each log just before you sew it rather than ahead of time.

**Round 1**

Log 1: Do not trim.

Log 2: Trim ½" from the short end.

Log 3: Trim ½" from the short end.

Log 4: Trim 1" from the short end.

**Round 2**

Log 1: Trim 1" from the short end.

Log 2: Trim 1½" from the short end.

Log 3: Trim 1½" from the short end.

Log 4: Trim 2" from the short end.

**Round 3**

Log 1: Trim 2" from the short end.

Log 2: Trim 2½" from the short end.

Log 3: Trim 2½" from the short end.

Log 4: Trim 3" from the short end.

4. Repeat step 3 for round 1, logs 3 and 4. If you're trimming as you go, measure each unit and trim the new log to that length before sewing. Press seam allowances toward the new logs.

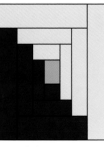

5. Repeat steps 3 and 4 to add round 2 and round 3.

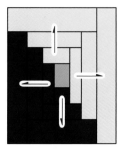

6. Repeat steps 1–5 to make 56 blocks.

7. Separate the blocks into two stacks: one stack with blocks that have three dark corners, and one stack with blocks that have three light corners.

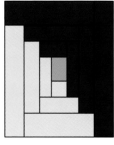

3 light corners            3 dark corners

## ASSEMBLY

1. Arrange the blocks into seven vertical rows of eight blocks each, alternating blocks from each stack as shown below. Arrange the blocks so that identical prints are not side by side. View your arrangement from a distance using my "10-foot rule" (page 5) to check the visual balance.

2. Sew the blocks into horizontal rows. Press seam allowances from row to row in alternating directions.

3. Sew the rows together into four sets of two each. Press the seam allowances in opposite directions from row to row. Combine the sets and press seam allowances in one direction.

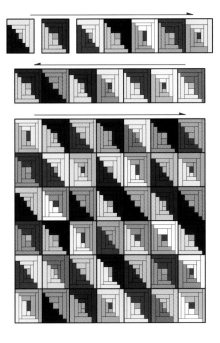

## ADDING BORDERS

Refer to "Borders" on page 9 as needed.

1. Sew the green checked strips together end to end to make one long strip.

2. Fold the long border strip in half lengthwise, matching short ends. Vertically center the folded border directly under the quilt top and trim the border strip even with the edges of the quilt top.

3. Pin and sew the borders to the sides of the quilt. Press the seam allowances toward the borders.

4. Repeat steps 2 and 3, centering the border strip horizontally under the quilt top, to cut and add the top and bottom borders.

5. Repeat steps 1–4 using the pink polka-dot strips to make and attach the outer border.

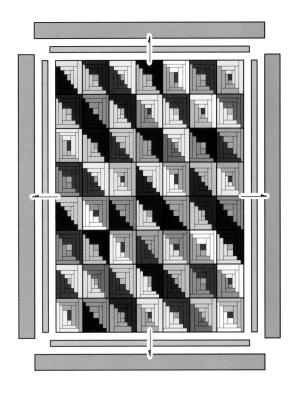

## FINISHING

Refer to "Finishing the Quilt" on page 9 as needed.

1. Divide the backing fabric crosswise into two equal panels, each approximately 90" long. Remove the selvages and sew the pieces together along a long edge to make a backing piece approximately 71" x 90"; press the seam allowances to one side.

2. Layer the quilt top with the batting and backing, keeping the backing seam parallel to the long edges of the quilt top. Baste the layers together using your favorite method.

3. Hand or machine quilt as desired. My quilt was long-arm quilted with a medium-sized stipple pattern.

4. Trim the backing and batting even with the edges of the quilt top and use the 2½"-wide strips to bind the quilt.

# CRITICAL (STASH) MASS

I always love to work from my stash and tend to become uneasy when it suddenly builds up. I took a look at my stash and determined it had reached "critical mass" (the amount of something required to maintain a venture or chain reaction) and determined it was time to begin the venture! I previewed colors until I decided on a purple-and-green theme, and then went about pulling those colors from my stash. I like to design blocks without too much predetermined outcome, but with enough consistency that I do maintain some control in the final layout. With this quilt, the blocks will either have a purple or a green edge, making it slick for a purple-and-green block layout. So as not to be too consistent, I designed two different-sized center squares, which are both off-center. I resisted the temptation to cut my sets with curvy or crooked lines—perhaps you want to give it a try. I know I will eventually.

## MATERIALS

⅔ yard *each* of 6 different purple prints for blocks

⅔ yard *each* of 6 different green prints for blocks

½ yard of black-and-white print for large (block 2) centers

½ yard of dark purple for inner border

¼ yard of different black-and-white print for small (block 1) centers

⅔ yard of fabric for binding

5¼ yards of fabric for backing

73" x 92" piece of batting

### fabric tips

I chose two colorways with this quilt: green and purple. For the purple prints, I strayed from violet to a bluish purple to dark purple. For the green prints, I used lime green as well as medium green. I found a lot of my batiks and tone-on-tone fabrics worked great together for this quilt.

Finished Quilt: 62½" x 82½" • Finished Block: 48 blocks, 10" x 10"
Pieced and quilted by Karla Alexander

# CUTTING

*All measurements include ¼" seam allowances.*

**From *each* of the 6 different purple prints, cut:**

2 strips, 4" x 42"; cut each strip into 2 strips, 4" x 20" (24 total)

1 strip, 5½" x 42"; cut into 2 strips, 5½" x 20" (12 total)

1 strip, 6½" x 42"; cut into 2 strips, 6½" x 20" (12 total)

**From *each* of the 6 different green prints, cut:**

2 strips, 4" x 42"; cut each strip into 2 strips, 4" x 20" (24 total)

1 strip, 5½" x 42"; cut into 2 strips, 5½" x 20" (12 total)

1 strip, 6½" x 42"; cut into 2 strips, 6½" x 20" (12 total)

**From the black-and-white print for block 1, cut:**

2 strips, 3" x 42"; cut into 24 squares, 3" x 3"

**From the black-and-white print for block 2, cut:**

3 strips, 4" x 42"; cut into 24 squares, 4" x 4"

**From the dark purple fabric, cut:**

8 strips, 1¾" x 42"

**From the binding fabric, cut:**

8 strips, 2½" x 42"

## MAKING THE BLOCKS

Refer to "Stack the Deck Blocks" on page 6 as needed.

1. With right sides up, arrange and neatly stack three purple 4"-wide strips alternately with three green 4"-wide strips to make eight decks of six strips each. Every deck should have a variation of fabrics without any duplicate prints. Alternating purple and green, stack the 5½"-wide strips in four decks of six strips each and the 6½"-wide strips in four decks of six strips each. Secure the decks with a pin through all layers until ready to sew.

2. Work with one deck at a time. Use a ruler to measure and cut lengthwise through the deck two times, dividing the deck into three long strips. When making your cuts, make sure your narrowest strip is never less than 1¼" wide. Vary the width of the cuts from deck to deck, trying to make each one different from the next.

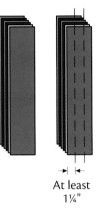

At least
1¼"

3. Peel the top strip from the center stack and place it on the bottom of that stack. Peel the top two strips off the right stack and place them on the bottom of that stack. Do not shuffle the stack on the left.

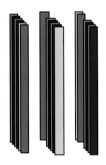

4. Chain piece the left strips to the center strips. (See "Chain Piecing" on page 7.) Clip the thread after the last strips are sewn and pull the entire unit back toward you until you reach the first set. Open the units up and add the right strip to the combined strips to make a strip set. Press seam allowances to one side. In the same manner, make strip sets from all of the decks. You will have three different widths of strip sets; 3"-wide, 4½"-wide, and 5½"-wide.

5. Use each strip set from step 4 to cut rectangles as indicated in the chart below until you have 24 of each unit. Units A–D are for block 1 and units E–H are for block 2. Sort each group of units into two stacks, one with purple side strips and one with green side strips.

| Block 1 unit | Strip set width | Cut 2 rectangles |
|---|---|---|
| A | 3" | 3" x 8" |
| B | 3" | 3" x 5½" |
| C | 5½" | 5½" x 5½" |
| D | 5½" | 5½" x 8" |

| Block 2 unit | Strip set width | Cut 2 rectangles |
|---|---|---|
| E | 3" | 3" x 8" |
| F | 3" | 3" x 6½" |
| G | 4½" | 4½" x 6½" |
| H | 4½" | 4½" x 8" |

6. Begin with block 1 units with purple side strips. Arrange one A unit, one B unit, one C unit, and one D unit with a 3" x 3" center square as shown.

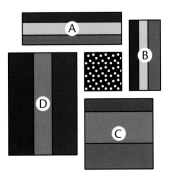

7. Refer to the diagram following step 11 as needed for block assembly. Sew the A unit to the center square, starting at the top and stopping after sewing about 1" to make a partial seam. Open the unit and finger-press the seam allowances away from the 3" square.

8. Rotate the block 90° so that unit A is at the top. Sew the B unit to the entire length of the right side. Open the unit and finger-press the seam allowances away from the center square.

9. Rotate the block 90° so that unit B is at the top. Sew the C unit to the entire length of the right side. Open the unit and finger-press the seam allowances away from the center square.

10. Rotate the block 90° so that unit C is at the top. Fold the A unit out of the way. Sew the D unit to the entire length of the right side. Open the unit and finger-press the seam allowances away from the center square.

11. Flip the block over so the seam allowances are facing you. Complete the partial seam in the center square by sewing over the last few stitches at the end of the original seam and out to the edge of unit D. Press the seam allowances away from the center square.

12. Repeat steps 7–12 to make 12 of block 1 with purple edges. Repeat again, using the block 1 units with green side strips to make 12 of block 1 with green edges (24 total of block 1). In the same manner, use the E, F, G, and H units and the 4" x 4" squares to make 12 of block 2 with purple edges and 12 of block 2 with green edges (24 total of block 2).

Block 1
with purple edges.
Make 12.

Block 1
with green edges.
Make 12.

Block 2
with purple edges.
Make 12.

Block 2
with green edges.
Make 12.

## ASSEMBLY

1. Arrange block 1 into four horizontal rows of six blocks each. Alternate green-edged blocks with purple-edged blocks. Twist and turn the blocks until you are pleased with the arrangement.

2. Place block 2 on the outside edges to create the outer border. Alternate green-edged blocks with purple-edged blocks. Twist and turn the blocks until you are pleased with the arrangement. View your arrangement using the "10-foot rule" on page 5.

3. For the inside portion of the quilt, sew block 1 together in rows. (Do not sew block 2 at this time.) Press the seam allowances in opposite directions from row to row. Sew the rows together and press the seam allowances in one direction.

4. Sew the 1¾"-wide purple strips together end to end to make one long strip for the inner border. From this long strip cut two strips 1¾" x 60½", two strips 1¾" x 63", and four rectangles 1¾" x 10½".

5. Sew the six middle blocks for the left side border together; press seam allowances in one direction. Repeat for the right border.

6. Sew a 1¾" x 60½" purple strip to each side of the quilt top. Press seam allowances toward the purple strips. Add the block borders from step 5 to each side of the quilt top. Press all seam allowances toward the purple strip.

7. Sew the 1¾" x 63" purple strips to the top and bottom of the quilt top; press the seam allowances toward the purple strip.

8. Sew the six middle blocks for the top border together; press seam allowances in one direction. Repeat for the bottom border. Sew a 1¾" x 10½" purple rectangle to each end of the top and bottom borders. Press seam allowances toward the purple rectangles.

9. Add the corner blocks to each end of the top and bottom border units; press seam allowances toward the purple rectangles. Sew the top and bottom borders to the quilt. Press seam allowances toward the inner border.

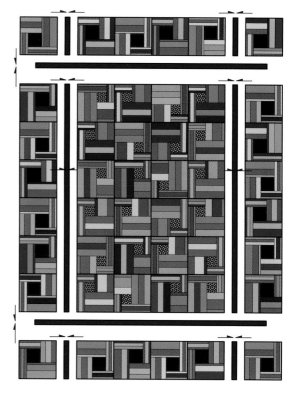

## FINISHING

Refer to "Finishing the Quilt" on page 9 as needed.

1. Divide the backing fabric crosswise into two equal panels, each approximately 92" long. Remove the selvages and sew the pieces together along the long edges to make a backing piece approximately 73" x 92"; press.

2. Layer the quilt top with the batting and backing, keeping the backing seam parallel to the long edges of the quilt top. Baste the layers together using your favorite method.

3. Hand or machine quilt as desired. I machine quilted a diagonal grid (approximately 60°) with random intervals of 2", 3", and 4" apart.

4. Trim the backing and batting even with the edges of the quilt top and use the 2½"-wide strips to bind the quilt.

# SQUARE ADAPTATIONS

With this quilt, you have your hands on the designing wheel. You can make your quilt a different size than mine. You can choose how many blocks to make by how many squares you begin with, or you can start with larger squares. What's really awesome is that you can use this method with any squares 5" x 5" and larger. You can precut all your squares to size (assuming your ¼" seam allowance is accurate) or you can trim as you sew so that all your blocks will be the exact same size, making for easy quilt construction.

## MATERIALS

*All yardages are based on 42"-wide fabric.*

280 assorted squares, 5" x 5", from a variety of contrasting fabrics, or ⅜ yard each of 18 contrasting small-scale prints

⅝ yard of binding fabric

3½ yards of backing fabric

59" x 80" piece of batting

## fabric tips

I started with a simple "charm pack" of 40 squares; these packs are available in most quilt stores. I had so much fun with these little squares, before I knew it I had assembled 216 blocks in variations of Four Patch and Square-in-a-Square blocks. If you don't have access to charm squares or aren't charmed by any of the choices, gather lots of your contrasting fabrics together and go for it. I consider 18 different fabrics the minimum number needed.

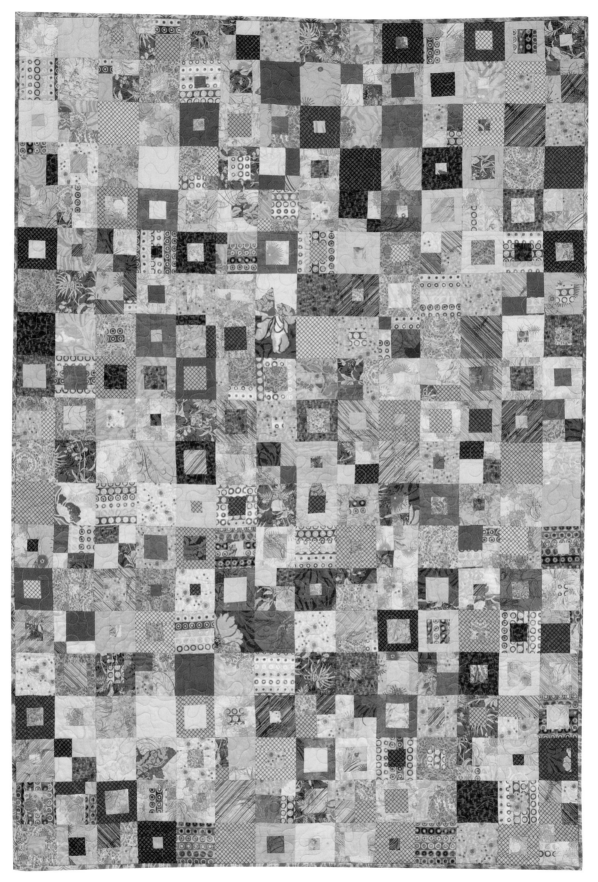

Finished Quilt: 49" x 70"  •  Finished Block: 280 blocks, 3½" x 3½"
Pieced by Karla Alexander, quilted by Dave Suderman

## CUTTING

*All measurements include ¼" seam allowances.*

If you're cutting your own fabrics instead of using precut squares, I suggest you begin by cutting all your squares 5". This way you can easily cut pieces for the Four Patch blocks and the plain squares to match the size of your sewn Square-in-a-Square blocks. If you want to precut all your pieces, I've also given the measurements for "perfectly" sewn blocks.

**From *each* of the 18 different fabrics, cut *either*:**

2 strips, 5" x 42"; cut each strip into 8 squares, 5" x 5" (288 total; you will use only 280)

***Or:***

9 squares, 5" x 5" (162 total; you will need only 160)

3 squares, 4½" x 4½" (54 total)

3 or 4 squares, 4" x 4" (66 total)

**From the binding fabric, cut:**

7 strips, 2½" x 42"

## MAKING THE BLOCKS

This quilt consists of two different pieced blocks: a Square-in-a-Square and a Four Patch, along with unpieced squares. Have fun designing your own quilt by adding or subtracting how many of each type of block you use. I've given instructions for the quantity of each in my quilt, but if you make a few more of each type, you'll give yourself more design options.

I suggest that you pretreat squares with your favorite spray sizing to help prevent distortion while sewing.

When you arrange your fabrics into decks, alternate each layer with a fabric that contrasts with the layer below. The final pieced blocks will always have a good balance of contrast.

### making the square-in-a-square blocks

Refer to "Stack the Deck Blocks" on page 6 as needed.

1.  Arrange 160 assorted 5" x 5" squares, right sides up, into 40 decks of 4 squares each, alternating contrasting prints. Each deck should have a different mix of fabric. Secure each deck with a pin through all the layers.

2.  Working with one deck at a time, decide on a measurement, no narrower than 1¼" and no wider than 2". Measure this distance from each side of the deck and cut vertically as shown. Slide the side stacks away from the center stack. Measure the same distance from the top and bottom of the center stack and cut horizontally as shown.

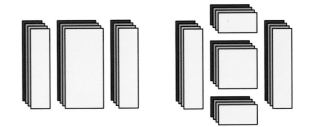

3.  Shuffle the center square by peeling the top fabric off the stack and placing it on the bottom of that stack.

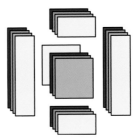

4.  Starting with the top layer, chain piece the small upper pieces to the center squares as shown below. (See "Chain Piecing" on page 7.) Repeat with the small lower pieces. Press seam allowances away from the center. Restack the units in the exact order in which they were shuffled.

5.  Measure the length of the units from step 4. Trim the unsewn pieces to this exact length. If your seam allowance is a precise ¼", you will always trim 1". Sew the last two pieces to opposite sides of the center unit. Press the seam allowances toward the added units.

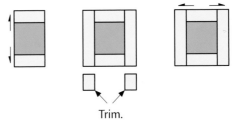

Trim.

6.  Repeat steps 2–5 with the remaining decks. Make the cuts on each deck the same width, but vary the widths from deck to deck. A narrow cut edge creates a large center square. A wide cut edge makes a small center square. If you want a quilt with a more uniform look than mine, another option is to make the cuts in all the decks the same width.

### karla's tip

Cut and sew one deck at a time. This way you can preview what your cuts look like and determine how to cut the next deck. When you preview your blocks, remember that the side pieces will be ¼" narrower in the sewn quilt top.

## making the four patch blocks

1.  If starting with 5" squares, you have the option of "custom fitting" the Four Patch blocks to your Square-in-a-Square blocks. Measure your Square-in-a-Square blocks to find the size of the smallest one. Add ½" to that measurement and trim 54 assorted 5" squares to that size. If sewn perfectly, the Square-in-a-Square blocks should measure 4" x 4" and you would trim the 5" squares to 4½" x 4½". You can also skip the measuring step and simply trim 54 assorted squares to 4½" x 4½".

2.  Arrange squares right sides up into 13 decks of four squares each and 1 deck of two squares, alternating contrasting prints. Each deck should have a different mix of fabrics. Secure each deck with a pin through all layers.

3.  Work with one deck at a time. Decide on a measurement, no narrower than 1¾" and no wider than 2½". Measure this distance from the right edge of the deck and cut vertically through all

layers as shown. Measure the same distance from the bottom edge of the deck and cut horizontally as shown.

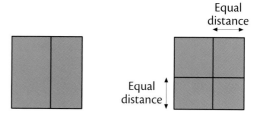

4.  Shuffle the deck by peeling the top fabric from the upper-right stack and placing it on the bottom of that stack. Peel the top two fabrics from the lower-left stack and place them on the bottom of that stack. For variety, I also shuffled the fabrics in the lower-right stack in a couple of the decks. To do this, first shuffle the upper-right and lower-left stacks as above. In addition, shuffle the lower-right stack by peeling the top three fabrics and moving them to the bottom of that stack. This will make a Four Patch block with four different fabrics.

5.  Starting with the top layer, chain piece the fabrics in the two upper stacks together. Press the seam allowances in one direction and restack in the exact shuffled order. In the same manner, chain piece the fabrics in the two lower stacks together. Press the seam allowances in the opposite direction and restack in the exact shuffled order. Sew the top units to the bottom units, matching the center seam. Press seam allowances to one side.

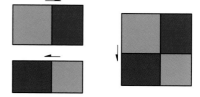

SQUARE ADAPTATIONS

6. Repeat steps 3–5 with the remaining decks to make 54 Four Patch blocks. Make the cuts on each deck the same width, but vary the widths from deck to deck. Shuffle the two-fabric deck by peeling the top fabric from the upper-right stack and placing it on the bottom of that stack. Peel the top fabric from the lower-left stack and place it on the bottom of that stack.

## ASSEMBLY

1. Measure your pieced blocks. If sewn perfectly, they should measure 4" x 4". It's OK if your blocks are different sizes! Simply trim all your blocks to match the size of your smallest square. Cut 66 squares from the assorted fabrics the same size as your blocks.

2. Arrange the pieced blocks and unpieced squares into 14 vertical rows of 20 blocks each. Arrange the blocks so that identical prints are not side by side, turning the blocks or moving them around until you're satisfied with the arrangement. Use my "10-foot rule" (page 5) to check for visual balance.

3. Sew the blocks into horizontal rows. Press seam allowances in alternating directions from row to row.

4. Sew the rows together into 10 sets of two rows each. Combine the sets into 5 sets of four rows each. Combine the sets and press the seam allowances in one direction.

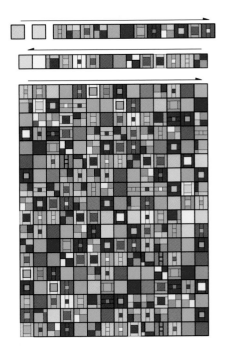

## FINISHING

Refer to "Finishing the Quilt" on page 9 as needed.

1. Divide the backing fabric crosswise into two equal panels, each approximately 59" long. Remove the selvages and sew the pieces together along a long edge to make a backing piece approximately 59" x 80"; press the seam allowances to one side.

2. Layer the quilt top with the batting and backing, keeping the backing seam parallel to the short edges of the quilt top. Baste the layers together using your favorite method.

3. Hand or machine quilt as desired. My quilt was long-arm quilted with a medium-sized stipple pattern.

4. Trim the backing and batting even with the edges of the quilt top and use the 2½"-wide strips to bind the quilt.

# ABOUT THE AUTHOR

Karla Alexander, quiltmaker, teacher, and author, has written four previous books; this is her fifth book on the art of quiltmaking. Karla has contributed her designs to Martingale & Company's yearly wall calendars, the *Creative Quilt Collection Volume Two*, as well as *More Skinny Quilts and Table Runners*.

She has also developed her own quilt design business, Saginaw Street Quilt Company, which offers a line of more than 50 different designs (www.saginawstreetquilts.com). She enjoys creating designs that enable the maker to reason out the cuts and placement of blocks for themselves, making the final result truly unique to each quilter. Karla also believes that beautiful doesn't have to be difficult, and specializes in techniques that are doable to the average or beginning quilter with just some good old-fashioned practice.

Karla lives in Salem, Oregon, with her husband, Don; the youngest of their three sons, William; and Lucy, the almost-black Lab.